THE YEAR YOU WERE BORN

MW00445316

1960

A fascinating book about the year 1960 with information on Events of the year, Adverts of 1960, Cost of living, Births, Sporting events, Book publications, The Oscars, Movies, Music, World events and People in power.

INDEX

US EVENTS OF 1960

January

2 | At the Senate Caucus room in Washington, U.S. Senator John F. Kennedy of Massachusetts formally announced that he would seek the Democratic nomination for President of the United States. Addressing a question about whether being a Roman Catholic would affect his chances of winning; Senator Kennedy told "I would think that there is really only one issue involved in the whole question of a candidate's religion, that is, does a candidate believe in the separation of church and state?"

3 | The CBS Sports Spectacular made its debut at 3:00 EST, with Bud Palmer, with the aim of showing "sports you seldom see". The first show featured a complete game between basketball's Harlem Globetrotters and their foils at that time, the Baltimore Rockets.

4 | The steel strike of 1959 was settled, three weeks before an injunction under the Taft-Hartley Act was set to expire, as Labor Secretary James P. Mitchell and Vice-President Richard M. Nixon mediated the dispute between the United Steelworkers Association and eleven steel manufacturers.

5 | The Massachusetts Supreme Court ruled that a trust fund, set up by Benjamin Franklin's will in 1791 to assist "young married artificers", could not be divided before its 1991 maturity date, despite the fact that there were no more artificers who would benefit. Started by Franklin with the deposit of 1,000 pounds sterling, the fund had grown to $1,578,098 by 1960. By the time the monies were split between Massachusetts and Pennsylvania in 1991, the Fund was worth more than $6.5 million.

6 | At the Johns Hopkins University Hospital in Baltimore, an emergency room intern, Dr. Henry Thomas, became the first person to save a life following CPR training. The technique of "closed chest compression" had been shown to Dr. Thomas and other physicians by developed by Dr. James Jude, but had only been attempted before during surgery. The patient, 45-year-old Eugene Barnes, had collapsed while removing his shirt for an examination. Dr. Thomas applied cardiopulmonary resuscitation and kept Barnes alive during a 22-minute wait for a defibrillator, and Barnes went on to a full recovery. The rest of the world would learn about CPR in the July 9, 1960, issue of the Journal of the American Medical Association.

7 | For the first time, a Polaris missile reached its target using its own inertial guidance system, rather than being directed from a ground station. The shot from Cape Canaveral came a few hours after President Eisenhower's final State of the Union speech, describing the new era of nuclear submarines armed with the Polaris missiles. "Impossible to destroy by surprise attack," said Ike, "they will become one of our most effective sentinels for peace."

8 | The Los Angeles Rams sued the new American Football League and the Houston Oilers over the rights to Heisman Trophy winner Billy Cannon, who had signed with both teams.

9 | On his 47th birthday, Vice-President Richard M. Nixon became a candidate for the Republican nomination for the President of the United States, by giving his assent to the placing of his name on the ballot for primary elections in Oregon, New Hampshire and Ohio.

11 | Henry Lee Lucas, who would confess to more than 600 murders in 1985, then recant, took his first life, stabbing his 74-year-old mother, Viola, at her home in Tecumseh, Michigan. Sentenced to 40 years in prison, but released in 1970, Lucas then resumed killing, and was ultimately convicted of 11 homicides.

13 | The first discussions were held in the White House to discuss covert action to overthrow Cuba's new revolutionary socialist government led by prime minister Fidel Castro. A special group, created by the National Security Council's order #5412, approved "Operation Zapata".

15 | Eight Chicago policemen were arrested in early morning raids on their homes, and charged with burglary, and several carloads of stolen merchandise were seized from the homes. By the end of the month, 15 city cops had been indicted for what Mayor Daley called "the most disgraceful and shocking scandal in the police department's history. The arrests followed a revelation, by a 23-year-old burglar, that several members of the Chicago PD had assisted him in burglarizing businesses in areas they had been assigned to patrol.

17 | It was announced that U.S. President Dwight D. Eisenhower would make a ten-day tour of the Soviet Union from June 10 to June 19, 1960, as the guest of Soviet First Secretary Nikita S. Khrushchev.[38] The visit would never take place, and was called off after the U-2 incident in May.

19 | The Treaty of Mutual Cooperation and Security between the United States and Japan was signed at the White House by signed by U.S. President Eisenhower and Japan's Prime Minister Kishi. Unpopular in Japan, the treaty was ratified there in June, and Kishi resigned soon afterward.

22 | At the Boston Garden, Sugar Ray Robinson lost his world middleweight boxing title in an upset to Paul Pender, a 29-year-old firefighter from Brookline, Massachusetts. Pender outpointed Robinson in fifteen rounds.

23 | Undersea explorer Jacques Piccard, and Navy Lt. Don Walsh, descended in the U.S. Navy bathyscaphe Trieste into the deepest depths of the ocean, reaching the bottom of the Mariana Trench in the Pacific, a depth of more than seven miles.

25 | Wilt Chamberlain set an NBA record that still stands, for "Most points, rookie, game", with 58 points for the Philadelphia Warriors against the Detroit Pistons, in Bethlehem, PA.

26 | After 22 ballots to select the new National Football League Commissioner, Marshall Leahy had seven votes, Austin Gunsel had four, but neither candidate had the required 10 of 12 majority needed for the 12-team league. The compromise was the little-known general manager of the Los Angeles Rams, 33-year-old Pete Rozelle. Rozelle would go on to lead the NFL to become the most popular professional sports league in the United States.

28 | The 12-team NFL expanded for the first time since 1949, awarding the franchise for the Dallas Cowboys for 1960 and for the Minnesota Vikings for 1961.

Dallas Cowboys   **Minnesota Vikings**

30 | The American Football League filled out its eight teams by voting on where to place the franchise that had formerly been reserved for Minneapolis. Although a majority preferred to place an AFL team in Atlanta, the owners agreed that a second California team was needed, and the team became the Oakland Raiders.

February

3 | U.S. President Eisenhower announced at a news conference that the United States should be able to make nuclear weapons available to its allies. Eisenhower urged that the Atomic Energy Act be amended in order to permit the U.S. to transfer weapons to the arsenals of other nations.

7 | Democratic presidential candidate John F. Kennedy was introduced by Frank Sinatra to Judith Campbell Exner. JFK and Exner had their first sexual encounter on March 7 at Room 1651 of the Plaza Hotel in New York.

8 | The Hollywood Walk of Fame was dedicated, starting with 1,558 names placed on terrazzo stars along Hollywood Boulevard in Hollywood, California, as an urban renewal program.

11 | The bodies of five crewmembers of the B-24 Liberator Lady Be Good were located by exploration worker James Backhaus, in the Libyan desert; 16 years after the airplane had vanished on April 4, 1943, during the Second World War. The men had walked 85 miles in hopes of finding help, before running out of water.

16	The nuclear submarine USS Triton submerged upon departure from New London, Connecticut, and, with 184 people on board, began an underwater trip around the world that ended 83 days later on May 10. The Triton was forced to broach its sail above the surface on March 5 in order to transfer a seriously ill sailor to another ship, and then spent the rest of the circumnavigation entirely undersea.
18	The 1960 Winter Olympics were opened in Squaw Valley, California, by U.S. Vice-President Richard M. Nixon, despite severe winter weather that kept away most of the spectators. The Games attracted 740 athletes from 30 nations.
19	Physician Barbara Moulton resigned in protest from the U.S. Food and Drug Administration, writing a letter to Commissioner George P. Larrick that included the accusation that the FDA had "failed utterly in its solemn task of enforcing those sections of the law dealing with the safety and misbranding of drugs".
23	Demolition began at Brooklyn's Ebbets Field, home of baseball's Dodgers until their move to Los Angeles in 1958. A crowd of 200 fans and former Brooklyn players watched as Lucy Monroe sang the National Anthem at Ebbets for the last time, and a band played Auld Lang Syne. The wrecking ball, painted white and painted to resemble a giant baseball, began its work with the destruction of the visitors' dugout.

24	The United States tested its first intercontinental ballistic missile (ICBM). Launched from Cape Canaveral, the Titan missile traveled 5,000 miles and ejected a data capsule before crashing into the South Atlantic.
29	St. Louis radio station KMOX revolutionized radio with the debut of a live call-in program called At Your Service.

March

1 NASA established an Office of Life Sciences to work on exobiology, based on Dr. Joshua Lederberg's ideas that space vehicles should be sterilized before and after their missions in order to prevent the possibility of contamination of outer space or of the Earth by microbes.

3 Lucille Ball filed for a divorce from Desi Arnaz. Television's Lucy and Ricky had filmed their last show together three weeks earlier. While I Love Lucy had ended in 1957, the couple had appeared later in 13 one-hour specials airing under the title The Lucy–Desi Comedy Hour.

5 Staff Sergeant Elvis Presley was honorably discharged from active service in the United States Army, nearly two years after being drafted into the service on March 24, 1958. After departing from Fort Dix in New Jersey, Presley remained in the U.S. Army reserve for four additional years until completing his military obligations.

6 President Eisenhower announced that 3,500 American troops would be posted to South Vietnam.

9 The Scribner shunt, a flexible Teflon tube that could be permanently implanted to connect an artery to a vein, was first implanted into a human patient. For the first time, persons with kidney failure could receive dialysis on a regular basis. Prior to the shunt's invention by Dr. Belding H. Scribner, glass tubes had to be inserted into blood vessels every time that dialysis was given. As one observer noted, "Scribner took something that was 100% fatal and overnight turned it into a condition with a 90% survival." The historic operation took place at the University of Washington hospital, and 39-year-old machinist Clyde Shields was the first beneficiary. At the same time, a new issue in bioethics was created, since decisions had to be made about which patients would be selected to receive the lifesaving treatment.

10 The first mitral valve replacement was performed on a 16-year-old girl, who had implanted in her prosthesis, made of polyurethane and Dacron, and designed by Drs. Nina Braunwald and Andrew Morrow. The girl survived the operation, but died 60 hours later. The next day, a 44-year-old woman received the valve and made a full recovery eight weeks later.

The first implantation of the caged ball heart valve, developed by Drs. Dwight E. Harken and William C. Birtwell, was made on Mary Richardson, who survived for 30 years after the surgery.

14 Richard Bissell, who oversaw the CIA's U-2 spy plane program, was warned by his aide, USAF Col. William Burke, that the Soviets had developed the missile capability to shoot down the high altitude (70,000 feet) U-2. Nevertheless, the spy flights continued, and on May 1, 1960, a U-2 would be downed in Soviet territory.

16 At a cave in Starved Rock State Park near Ottawa, Illinois, the bodies of three women were found. All three, residents of Riverside, Illinois, and the wealthy wives of Chicago business executives, had been beaten to death two days before, during an afternoon of birdwatching. A dishwasher at the park later confessed to killing the women after attempting to rob them. Chester Weger, convicted of the murder, was sentenced to life imprisonment, and was denied parole as recently as December 2009.

17 Following a 2:30 meeting at the White House with Allen Dulles and Richard Bissell of the CIA, President Eisenhower authorized the agency to train and equip Cuban exiles to overthrow the regime of Fidel Castro, an operation which would become, in 1961, the Bay of Pigs Invasion.

18 | The "Snark missile" began its brief service as a nuclear tipped American ICBM. Designed by Northrop and named after the Lewis Carroll poem, "The Hunting of the Snark", the 30 missiles were deployed at Presque Isle Air Force Base in Maine as part of the 702d Strategic Missile Wing. Fifteen months later, the Snarks were declared to be obsolete, and deactivated by order of President Kennedy.

22 | Arthur Leonard Schawlow and Charles H. Townes of Bell Labs received U.S. patent No. 2,929,922 for an optical maser, now more commonly referred to as the laser. Other scientists, including Gordon Gould, were working on their own discoveries for "light amplification by stimulated emission of radiation", and legal battles between Gould and Bell Labs continued for 28 years.

23 | Marty Dalton, 91, inmate of the Rhode Island State Prison in Cranston, Rhode Island, since 1897. Dalton had refused parole in 1930 after serving 33 years for the killing of a New York businessman, and after a two-hour tour of the outside world, asked to stay because the prison was his only home.

26 | The Minneapolis Lakers played their last NBA game, losing in Game 7 of the Western Conference playoffs, 97–86, to the St. Louis Hawks. The Lakers would move to Los Angeles during the off-season.

27 | The last regularly scheduled service in America, of a passenger train powered by a steam engine, took place when Grand Trunk Western Railroad ran a steam locomotive for the last time, on a route between Detroit and Durand, Michigan.

April

1 The United States launched the first weather satellite, the 270 pound TIROS-1, from Cape Canaveral at 6:40 a.m. EST. The name was an acronym for Television Infra-Red Observation Satellite. The same evening, satellite weather photos were introduced to the world, on television, for the first time. Taken from an altitude of 450 miles, the pictures of cloud cover confirmed the spiral pattern of winds in a storm.

4 At the 32nd Academy Awards ceremony, Ben Hur won a record eleven Oscars, including Best Picture.

5 The name for Oakland, California's new pro football team was announced. The Oakland Señors were renamed the "Raiders" nine days later.

10 The last successful American U-2 overflight of the Soviet Union took place, as a pilot passed near the missile range at Tyuratam. The S-75 Dvina missile batteries that could have downed the plane had not been alerted in time of the intrusion, and several Soviet senior commanders were fired. On May 1, a U-2 plane flown by Francis Gary Powers would be downed.

13 The United States launched Transit I-B, the first successful navigation satellite, at 7:03 EST from Cape Canaveral. The Transit technology was eventually superseded by Global Positioning System satellites, which were aided by Rudolf E. Kalman's development, later in the year, of the Kalman filter.

17 The Russwood Park baseball stadium in Memphis, Tennessee, burned to the ground shortly after Chicago White Sox vs Cleveland Indians game.

April

20 | Elvis Presley returned to Hollywood for the first time since his return from military service in Germany, to begin filming G.I. Blues.

24 | One of the first widely publicized stories of hysterical strength happened in Tampa, Florida, when Mrs. Florence Rogers, a 123-pound woman, lifted one end of a 3,600 pound car that had fallen off of a jack and onto her 16-year-old son, Charles Trotter. Mrs. Rogers, an LPN, fractured several vertebrae in the process.

27 | USS Tullibee (SSN-597), the first nuclear-powered electric-drive submarine, was launched from Groton, Connecticut. At 273 feet long and 2,640 tons displacement, USS Tullibee was the smallest nuclear-powered attack submarine in the US submarine fleet. The initial manning complement was 7 officers and 60 enlisted men. However before inactivation, the crew included 13 officers and over 100 enlisted men.

28 | The construction of what would become Shea Stadium, at Flushing, Queens, was approved by New York City's Board of Estimate, 20–2, giving the proposed Continental League the chance to launch. The Continental League never played, but the stadium gave the National League the impetus to return to the city, with the New York Mets.

May

1 The U-2 Incident began when an American U-2 spy plane, piloted by Francis Gary Powers, entered Soviet airspace ten minutes after takeoff from a U.S. base in Pakistan, at Peshawar. At 9:53 am (0653 GMT), his plane was struck by shrapnel from an exploding Soviet SA-2 missile while he was at 70,500 feet (21,488 m). Powers parachuted and chose not to commit suicide, and landed near Sverdlovsk, where he was captured alive.

2 Outfielder Jim Lemon of the Washington Senators became the first Major League Baseball player to wear a batting helmet with earflaps. Helmets had been required in both leagues since 1958 but the helmet, required in Little League Baseball, was made available by Senators' owner Calvin Griffith, who ordered the headgear after Earl Battey was struck in the head by a pitch thrown by Earl Battey of the Boston Red Sox. Despite concerns that the flap obscured the batter's vision, Lemon got two hits in three at-bats in a 3-2 win over the Cleveland Indians.

4 The United States signed an agreement to sell 17,000,000 metric tons of surplus grain to India over a four-year period, in exchange for $1,276,000,000.

9 The U.S. Food and Drug Administration approved a birth control pill for the first time, as it cleared the prescription of Enovid, manufactured by G. D. Searle & Company, for use as an oral contraceptive.

10 John F. Kennedy defeated Hubert Humphrey in the West Virginia primary election, winning the predominantly Protestant state and dispelling doubts about whether Americans would support a Roman Catholic nominee. The win was Senator Kennedy's seventh in the primaries. At 1:08 a.m. the next day, Humphrey conceded defeat, and then said "I am no longer a candidate for the Democratic Presidential nomination", leaving Senator Kennedy unopposed.

Hubert Humphrey

John F. Kennedy

May

11 At a press conference, President Eisenhower of the United States accepted full responsibility for the U-2 incident, and said that spying on the Soviet Union was justified. "No one wants another Pearl Harbor", he said, adding "In most of the world, no large-scale attack could be prepared in secret, but in the Soviet Union there is a fetish of secrecy, and concealment."

15 While in Paris with President Eisenhower on the first day of a summit with Soviet Premier Khrushchev, U.S. Secretary of Defense Thomas S. Gates, Jr. ordered a test of the American military alert system. Declassified documents would later show that Gates's order at 0033 UTC for "a high state of command readiness" was misunderstood, and that within half an hour, the U.S. Joint Chiefs of Staff placed troops worldwide at DEFCON 3 status. The American public learned of the alert when Lowry Air Force Base asked police to locate key personnel, and the police asked Denver radio station KOA (AM) and KOA-TV to assist. The message that followed- "All fighter pilots F-101 and fighter pilots F-102... Doe Three Alert, Hotcake One and Hotcake Six, scramble at Lowry immediately." was heard by thousands of Denver listeners.

17 "Radio Swan", secretly funded and operated by the American CIA, began broadcasting anti-Communist propaganda to Cuba, from a transmitter on Swan Island off of the coast of the Honduras.

24 The United States launched the Midas II satellite, the first designed to detect missile launches. "Midas" was an acronym for Missile Defense Alarm System.

26 At the United Nations in New York, U.S. Ambassador Henry Cabot Lodge, Jr. displayed a hand-carved replica of the Great Seal of the United States that had been presented by the Soviets as a gift to the American ambassador in Moscow, and the listening device that had been discovered inside "right under the beak of the eagle".

30 The 1960 Indianapolis 500 was won by Jim Rathmann. Prior to the race, temporary seating collapsed, killing two people and injuring 70.

June

2 For the first time since 1919, New York's 22 Broadway theaters were closed, and scheduled performances were cancelled. The "theater blackout" was occasioned by a dispute between the Actors Equity Association and the League of New York Theaters, but was resolved after eleven days.

5 Dwight D. Eisenhower became the first incumbent President of the United States to deliver the commencement speech at the University of Notre Dame. Jimmy Carter (1977), Ronald Reagan (1981), George H.W. Bush (1992), George W. Bush (2001) and Barack Obama (2009) were later speakers.

6 The first fixed-rate heart pacemaker, with five year mercuric-oxide battery and designed by a team headed by William Chardack, was implanted in a patient.

7 A BOMARC missile, and its nuclear warhead, caught fire at McGuire Air Force Base in New Jersey. Although a liquid helium tank in the missile exploded, and the warhead was melted by the fire, there was no risk of a nuclear blast in the Philadelphia area. The accident did cause a spillage of plutonium, and the contaminated areas were subsequently encased under asphalt and concrete.

June

10 In Tokyo, President Eisenhower's Press Secretary, James C. Hagerty, appointments secretary Thomas E. Stephens, and U.S. Ambassador to Japan Douglas MacArthur II had their car surrounded by an angry mob, and were trapped inside for an hour and a half before a U.S. Marine helicopter rescued them. Eisenhower set off on his tour of the Far East the next day and refused to postpone his trip to Japan.

15 A heat burst occurred near the resort of Lake Whitney, Texas, shortly after midnight, followed by a windstorm. Despite later claims that, from 80 degrees, "the temperature rose to nearly 140 °F", contemporary accounts at the time reported a peak of 95°.

17 El Rancho Vegas, which in 1941 became the first casino resort on what would become the Las Vegas Strip, burned down.

18 "Freedomland", a theme park designed in the shape of the United States and billed (until a lawsuit) as "Disneyland of the East", was dedicated in the Bronx, and opened the next day.

19 The Charlotte Motor Speedway opened in Concord, North Carolina, and hosted the first World 600 NASCAR race. Joe Lee Johnson won the first running of the 600.

20 At New York's Polo Grounds, a crowd of 31,892 watched Floyd Patterson became the first person to regain the world heavyweight boxing championship. In the fifth round, Patterson knocked out champion Ingemar Johansson with a powerful left hook that left the Swedish boxer unconscious for ten minutes. Johansson then walked out under his own power.

22 The first launch of two satellites from the same rocket took place at Cape Canaveral, as the United States placed a Transit II-A and a solar radiation satellite into space. Thirty minutes later, a spring-loaded device sent the two spheres into separate orbits.

28 Lightning strikes started 143 separate fires across Arizona and New Mexico, the most recorded in a single day.

29 The first weather satellite, TIROS, was shut down by NASA after 78 days, 1,302 orbits, and almost 23,000 weather photos.

2 | Former U.S. President Harry S. Truman said at a news conference in Independence, Missouri, that Democratic Party frontrunner John F. Kennedy lacked the maturity to be President, and that Kennedy should decline the nomination. Kennedy responded two days later, saying "I have encountered and survived every kind of hazard and opposition, and I do not intend to withdraw my name now, on the eve of the convention."

4 | For the first time, a 50-star flag of the United States was hoisted raised at 12:01 a.m. (EDT), at the Fort McHenry National Monument in Baltimore, and at the U.S. Capitol in Washington. At the time, there were only seven places in the United States where the national flag was permitted to be flown during hours of darkness.

9 | Rodger Woodward, a seven-year-old boy, became the first person known to survive an accidental plunge over Niagara Falls. Roger had been a passenger in a boat on the Niagara River, when the outboard motor failed. He fell 165 feet over the Falls, but sustained only minor bruises and a cut, and was released from a hospital two days later.

12 | The Etch A Sketch was first manufactured. Licensed to Ohio Art Company by French inventor André Cassagnes, it quickly became one of the most popular toys of all time.

18 | Two U.S. Navy destroyers, the USS Ammen and the USS Collett, collided off of the coast of Newport Beach, California, killing ten sailors.

July

20 The submarine USS George Washington made the first launch of a rocket from underwater into the air, with the firing of an unarmed Polaris missile while submerged at a depth of 30 feet.

26 Fifteen months after U.S. President Eisenhower had proposed that the Soviet Union and the United States be allowed to inspect their opponents' missile sites, the Soviets made a counteroffer "to allow international inspection teams to carry out three on-site inspections annually on its territory." The U.S. and its allies considered the number to be inadequate, but saw it as the basis for negotiations. Actual inspections would not take place until more than 25 years later.

30 The American Football League played its first game, an exhibition between the Buffalo Bills and the Boston Patriots, before a crowd of 16,474 in Buffalo, and the home team lost, 28 to 7. Bob Dee of the Patriots recovered a fumble in the end zone for the first unofficial AFL score.

August

2 The Continental League, proposed as a third major league for baseball, came to an end after CL President Branch Rickey and co-founder William Shea concluded a meeting in Chicago with representatives of the National League and American League. The NL and AL, each with eight teams, had been confronted with the proposed eight team CL. By agreement, each established league would place franchises in proposed CL cities. For 1962, three Continental sites had franchises, with the National League adding the New York Mets and the Houston Colt .45s (later the Astros), while the American League allowed its Washington Senators to relocate to the Minneapolis-St. Paul area as the Minnesota Twins. In later years, teams would be placed in Atlanta (1966), Dallas (1972), Toronto (1976) and Denver (1993). Buffalo, New York, was the only Continental site that would still be without a major league team nearly 60 years later.

4 NASA test pilot Joseph A. Walker became the fastest man in history as he flew an X-15 at a speed of 2,196 miles per hour, breaking a record set in 1956 by Milburn Apt, who had been killed while flying an X-2.

August

10 U.S. Navy frogmen successfully recovered the satellite Discoverer 13, marking the first retrieval of a satellite after twelve previous attempts had failed. Although plans to make the first mid-air capture failed, the recovery opened the era of the spy satellite.

12 Echo 1, the first communications satellite, was successfully launched by NASA. Weighing 137 pounds, Echo was a 100-foot-diameter (30 m) Mylar balloon, inflated after it reached orbit when the Sun's heat converted powders inside the balloon into gas. A pre-recorded message from U.S. President Eisenhower was transmitted from Goldstone, California, bounced off of Echo, and received at a station in Holmdel, New Jersey. The largest satellite launched up to that time, Echo was big enough that it could be seen from the Earth as it orbited at an average altitude of 1,000 miles.

16 Joseph Kittinger parachuted from a balloon over New Mexico at 102,800 feet (31,333 m). He set records, which stood for 52 years, for highest altitude jump; longest free-fall by falling 16 miles (25.7 km) over a period of 4 minutes and 38 seconds before opening his parachute; and fastest speed by a human without motorized assistance (320 mph). On October 14, 2012, Felix Baumgartner of Austria (using Kittinger as his adviser) would break all of Kittinger's records except for the longest duration for a free-fall, plunging 128,100 ft (39,045 m) in 4 minutes, 19 seconds.

August

18 The first photograph ever from a spy satellite was taken, after the launch of the American Discoverer 14 at 12:15 pm PDT, and showed a Soviet airfield at Mys Shmidta. With 3,000 feet of film, the satellite took more pictures than all 24 of the U-2 spy plane flights put together, and revealed the existence, not previously known to the U.S., of 64 airfields and 26 missile bases.

29 A 300 foot in diameter weather balloon, described by the U.S. Air Force as "the largest ever launched", crashed into a home in Stockton, California, an hour after being sent up from Vernalis Air Force Base. Mrs. Ben Petero evacuated her six children from the frame house after realizing that the balloon was descending on the family home.

30 John F. Kennedy appointed four "Cold War" aides in anticipation of his victory in the United States presidential election.

September

2 In the Summer Olympics, Wilma Rudolph, who had overcome childhood polio, won the women's 100 meter dash with a time of 11.0 seconds. Although faster than the world record of 11.3, Rudolph's mark was not official because the wind had been blowing faster than 2.0 m/s. Rudolph earned three golds, including the 200 m dash and the 4 × 100 m relay. In the long jump competition, Ralph Boston of the United States broke the Olympic record that had been set in 1936 by Jesse Owens. Boston was 4 inches short of the world record of 26 feet 11 3⁄4 inches (8.21 m) that he had set on August 12.

5 Cassius Clay of the United States (later Muhammad Ali), defeated Zbigniew Pietrzykowski of Poland to win the gold medal in the Olympic light heavyweight boxing competition. Franco De Piccoli of Italy was the Olympic heavyweight boxing medalist.

6 At the men's 400 meter dash, the Olympic record of 45.9 seconds was broken by the first four finishers. Otis Davis of the US and Carl Kaufmann of Germany were both credited with a new world record of 44.9 (with Davis winning gold by 0.02 seconds), Malcolm Spence of South Africa at 45.5, and Milkha Singh of India at 45.6.

9 The new American Football League made its debut with eight teams, as the visiting Denver Broncos defeated the Boston Patriots, 13 to 10. After barely surviving during its first four seasons, the AFL would merge with the older National Football League in 1966, bringing all of its teams (and two expansion teams) in to the NFL in 1970.

13 Lee Harvey Oswald's honorable discharge from the United States Marines, granted on September 11, 1959, was revised to an "undesirable discharge" (rather than a bad conduct discharge or a dishonorable discharge, which require a court martial), based on bringing "discredit to the Marine Corps through adverse newspaper publicity" since defecting to the Soviet Union. Although William B. Franke was the United States Secretary of the Navy at the time the revision was ordered, Oswald would not learn of the action until 1961, when John Connally was appointed to the position by President John F. Kennedy, and would write to Connally several times to seek a reversal. Connally would later win the office of Governor of Texas, and on November 22, 1963, Oswald would shoot both Kennedy and Connally; at least one author, James Reston Jr., would theorize that Oswald was actually trying to assassinate Governor Connally rather than President Kennedy.

September

21 | Dr. Albert Starr, along with Dr. Dwight Harken, performed the first successful implantation of an artificial mitral valve. The Starr-Edwards valve, designed by retired engineer Miles Edwards and Dr. Starr, was implanted into Philip Amundson, a 52-year-old farmer, in surgery at the University of Oregon. Amundson survived for ten years before dying in an accident.

24 | The Howdy Doody Show presented its 2,343rd and final episode, after a run that started on NBC on December 27, 1947. After the marionette Howdy Doody, and host Buffalo Bob Smith, gave their farewells, Clarabell the Clown— who had used pantomime and honking horns to communicate, but had never spoken— surprised his audience by saying, "Goodbye, kids."

25 | In baseball, the New York Yankees clinched the American League pennant with a 4–3 in over the Boston Red Sox. The day before, the Pittsburgh Pirates won the National League pennant for the first time in 33 years, despite a 4–2 loss to Milwaukee, after the St. Louis Cardinals were eliminated by a 5–0 loss to the Chicago Cubs.

26 | The two leading U.S. presidential candidates, Republican Richard M. Nixon and Democrat John F. Kennedy, participated in the first televised presidential debate, which took place in Chicago at the television studios of WBBM-TV. The one-hour-long event began at 8:30 pm local time. The first debate demonstrated the power of television in influencing voters. Kennedy appeared tan and charismatic, while Nixon, due in part to poor makeup and a recent hospitalization, looked unkempt and tense. A special act of Congress was passed in order to allow the American television and radio networks to broadcast the debate without having to provide equal time to other presidential candidates.

September

29 | My Three Sons made its television debut, with veteran film actor Fred MacMurray as the widowed father, Steve Douglas, and William Frawley (formerly Fred Mertz of I Love Lucy) as the boys' grandfather, "Bub" O'Casey. The series would air from 1960 to 1965 on ABC and from 1965 to 1972 on CBS, with numerous cast changes.

30 | At 8:30 pm EST, American television viewers were invited to meet The Flintstones, "a modern Stone Age family", with the premiere of the cartoon as a prime time series on ABC.

October

3 | Dwight D. Eisenhower became the oldest President of the United States, 11 days before turning 70, the age that Andrew Jackson had been on March 4, 1837. Eisenhower's record of 70 years, 98 days (on leaving office) would be broken by Ronald Reagan on May 15, 1981.

6 | James Tidwell was admitted to the Cincinnati General Hospital in Cincinnati, Ohio, for treatment of cancer, and became the first of 88 unwitting victims of an experiment by the University of Cincinnati and the Atomic Support Agency of the United States Department of Defense. On October 28, he would be subjected to his first of many doses of ionizing radiation over his entire body, starting at 100 rads, and increasing gradually to 250 rads, and on November 7, doses of 300 rads to his brain. He would die on November 29, 1960, 32 days after treatment began, the first fatality of the program, which would continue until 1971. The existence of the experiments would not be revealed to the public until 1994.

12 | A bomb explosion in Times Square subway station, New York City, injured 33 people. It was the third such bombing attack in eleven days.

13 | Three black mice were launched in an American rocket to an altitude of 700 miles, and recovered alive when the nose cone was recovered, becoming the first living creatures to survive a trip of that distance into outer space.

18 | Two American tourists, missing since a visit to the Soviet Union in August, were released unharmed and sent to Austria. Mark Kaminsky, 32, and Harvey Bennett, 26, had secretly been jailed in the Ukraine and tried by a military court for espionage. After pleading guilty, both men were deported.

19 | In Atlanta, Rev. Martin Luther King was arrested, along with 280 students, for taking part in a lunch counter sit-in at a Rich's department store. Charged with a parole violation from an earlier traffic violation, King was sentenced to four months of hard labor at the Reidsville State Prison, but released three days later after an appeal by Robert F. Kennedy, brother of Democratic presidential nominee John F. Kennedy, to Georgia Governor Ernest Vandiver.

20 | The price of gold rose sharply on the market in London, jumping by $3.00 per ounce after rises of 1 1/2, 8, and 26 1/2 cents in the first three days of the week. The price, which had been fixed by the United States at $35.20 per ounce since 1935, climbed past $40.00 on fears that the United States would devalue the dollar and that other nations' currencies would lose value as well. To avert a worldwide economic crisis, the United States Treasury increased its supply of gold to the Bank of England, and eight nations agreed not to buy gold for more than the fixed price.

23 | A woman in Milwaukee splashed Democratic candidate John F. Kennedy with whiskey while he was riding in an open convertible, then tossed the drinking glass into the car. According to an AP report, "Kennedy wiped his face, picked up the tumbler, said calmly 'here's your glass' and handed it back." No arrests were made. Kennedy would later be shot and killed while riding in an open convertible in Dallas.

25 | The first fully electronic wristwatch, the Accutron 214, was unveiled by the Bulova Watch Company, along with the tiny watch battery to power it. Promoting the watch as the "First instrument of the space age you can wear and use!" Bulova added "It doesn't even tick ... it hums!" The watch itself went on sale in jewelry stores on November 24, 1960 with the least expensive, stainless steel model retailing for $175, equivalent to $1,480 in 2018 dollars.

28 | Three American surgeons from the University of Vermont became the first persons to describe a new development in medicine, microvascular surgery or, more commonly, microsurgery. In an address to the gathering of the American Heart Association in St. Louis, Dr. Julius H. Jacobson II, told how he and two colleagues, Dr. Ernesto L. Suarez and Dr. Donald B. Miller, had successfully used an otologist's operating microscope, normally used for ear surgery, to successfully reconnect small blood vessels within a dog. Dr. Jacobson would later be referred to among vascular surgeons as "the father of microsurgery".

30 | Nine days before Election Day in the United States, Vice-President and Republican candidate Richard Nixon outraged President Dwight Eisenhower, at a White House luncheon, by pointedly refusing the President's offer to make campaign speeches in the final week. Eisenhower told RNC Chairman Len Hall, "Goddamnit, he looks like a loser to me."

November

1 President Eisenhower said that the United States would "take whatever steps are necessary" to defend the Guantanamo Naval Base in Cuba, "because of its importance to the defense of the entire hemisphere".

2 The recording by Elvis Presley of the song Are You Lonesome Tonight? Originally written in 1926, was released.

4 Filming of The Misfits, starring Clark Gable and Marilyn Monroe, was finished. It proved to be the last film for both legendary actors. Gable, who had performed many of his own stunts, had a heart attack the next day and died on November 16, Monroe would die in 1962 during the filming of the never completed Something's Got to Give.

8 In the U.S. presidential election, a record number of American voters turned out to make their choice between Democratic candidate and U. S. Senator John F. Kennedy and Republican candidate and U. S. Vice President Richard M. Nixon. With 270 electoral votes needed to win, Kennedy received 303. The popular vote was the closest in history. Kennedy (34,220,984) won slightly more than Nixon (34,108,157) by a margin of 1/6 of one percent of the total votes cast.

13 African-American singer and actor Sammy Davis, Jr. married white Swedish actress May Britt at a time when interracial marriage was uncommon, and, in some states, illegal. The resulting fallout would effectively end Britt's film career. The couple would have a daughter in 1961, and would adopt two sons, before separating in 1967 and divorcing in 1968.

November

15 | The submarine USS George Washington, armed with 16 nuclear-tipped Polaris missiles, sailed from the harbor of Charleston, South Carolina, following an undisclosed route. President Eisenhower praised history's first mobile nuclear missile base, noting that the Polaris firing submarines "possess a power and relative invulnerability which will make suicidal any attempt by an aggressor to attack the free world by surprise". The U.S. Navy said that the 16 missiles had the same destructive power as "the total of all of the bombs dropped during World War II". The Polaris has been described as "the world's most credible deterrent system".

24 | Wilt Chamberlain, of the Philadelphia Warriors, set the NBA record for number of rebounds (55) in a game, which has remained unbroken for nearly fifty years, but his team lost 132–129 to the visiting Boston Celtics, who were led by Bill Russell. Chamberlain's 55 rebounds broke the record of 51, set on February 8, 1959 by Bill Russell of the Boston Celtics. Chamberlain (23,924) and Russell (21,620) remain first and second on the all-time rebound list.

27 | The ABC television network first broadcast Issues and Answers, a Sunday morning interview show to compete with NBC's Meet the Press and CBS's Face the Nation.

30 | Ten days after the Chrysler Corporation announced that it was ceasing production of its Desoto line of automobiles; the very last Desoto was built. Chrysler had built an additional 300 after the announcement to fill orders.

December

2 | U.S. President Dwight D. Eisenhower authorized the use of $1M for the relief and resettlement of Cuban refugees, who had been arriving in Florida at the rate of 1,000 a week.

7 | The QH-50 DASH (Drone Anti-Submarine Helicopter), a drone that could be guided by remote control, made its first successful unmanned landing, descending upon the USS Hazelwood.

10 | The first underwater park within the United States, the John Pennekamp Coral Reef State Park, was formally dedicated. The park covers 178 square miles (460 km2) and protects coral reefs, seagrass, and mangroves inside its boundaries.

December

16 | In the collision of two airliners over New York City, 136 people were killed, including eight persons on the ground that were struck by falling debris. United Airlines Flight 826 from Chicago, with 77 passengers and seven crew, was outside its designated holding pattern for circling New York's Idlewild Airport, and collided with TWA Flight 266 5,200 feet (1,600 m) over Staten Island at 10:37am. The United DC-8 jet crashed in Brooklyn at the intersection of 7th Avenue and Sterling Place. Stephen Baltz, 11, was pulled conscious from the wreckage, but died the next day. The TWA plane, a Lockheed Super-Constellation with 39 passengers and five crew, had been on its way from Columbus, Ohio, to New York's La Guardia airport, and crashed on a vacant area at the Miller Field U.S. Army base on Staten Island. In addition to the 128 passengers and crew on both planes, eight more people on the streets of Brooklyn were killed by the falling debris.

19 | John F. Kennedy was elected as the 35th President of the United States, as the 534 persons who had been selected (on November 8) to serve in the Electoral College, met in their respective states' capitals. Democratic candidate Kennedy received 300 votes, 31 more than the 269 needed to win, and Republican challenger Richard M. Nixon had 219. U.S. Senator Harry F. Byrd received 15 votes, from all 8 of Mississippi's slate of unpledged electors (a ticket which finished ahead of Kennedy and Nixon), six from Alabama pledged to Kennedy and one from Oklahoma pledged to Nixon. Hawaii's 3 electors had not been certified, pending a recount of the popular vote, but were awarded to Kennedy prior to the January 6, 1961, tabulation.

26 | The Philadelphia Eagles defeated the Green Bay Packers, 17–13, to win the 1960 NFL championship. The AFL title game, between the Houston Oilers and the Los Angeles Chargers, would not take place until New Year's Day 1961.

29 | A former U.S. Defense Department employee was arrested by the FBI after taking almost 200 classified documents from the Weapons Systems Evaluation Group division at the Pentagon. Arthur Rogers Roddey, a mathematician who had top secret clearance, was sentenced to eight years in prison on March 22, 1961.

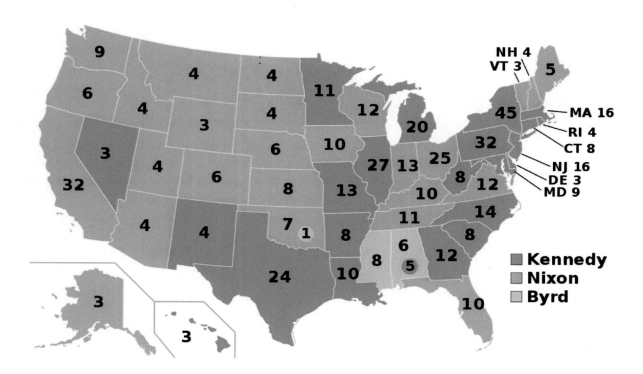

here for the
first time
anywhere—
elegance with economy

Impala Sport Coupe—one of 16 fresh-minted '60 Chevrolets you can choose from.

SUPERLATIVE '60 CHEVROLET

Here's new gem-bright beauty, new room to sprawl in and sit tall in. New lean-muscled engine economy, new spirit and silence in its going. For fineness of features, for precise craftsmanship— for all the things that make a car good to own—the '60 Chevrolet stands alone in its price field.

Just wait till you see it. Everything about the '60 Chevy, every styling accent, every engineering detail, has been polished and refined to a degree of perfection never before thought possible of a car in Chevrolet's price class.

Picture practicality and economy (there's even more of it in a new gas-saving V8!) combined with much of the luxury and hushed comfort usually associated with high-priced automobiles. That's Chevy for '60. Its overall effect is one of quiet elegance, a sophisticated new shape that embodies spacious inner dimensions. Space for long legs and broad shoulders, with sofa-wide seats and even more foot room for front seat passengers. Space that specializes in family travel!

Really, you have to see this one up close to appreciate its fresh beauty and fine workmanship. You have to take a turn behind the wheel to know its astonishing smoothness and almost total absence of road hum and vibration. We'll admit our enthusiasm's showing just a bit— but once you've dropped into your dealer's we're sure yours will be, too. *There's nothing like a new car—and there's never been a new car like this '60 Chevrolet!* . . . Chevrolet Division of General Motors, Detroit 2, Michigan.

NEAREST TO PERFECTION A LOW-PRICED CAR EVER CAME!

HOLIDAY/NOVEMBER

The Silver Age Green Lantern was created by John Broome and Gil Kane in Showcase #22 (October 1959) at the behest of editor Julius Schwartz. Volume 2 of Green Lantern began publication in August 1960. The series spotlighted the Silver Age Green Lantern, Hal Jordan and introduced the expansive mythology surrounding Hal's forbearers in the Green Lantern Corps.

FOR 1960

For *any* age ...for any type of two-wheeled FUN!

TRIUMPH
®

Introducing the heritage of british motorcycles

ICONIC 1960's

BONNEVILLE

T100

Triumph's legendary roadster

865cc parallel twin engine

Traditional styling looks

Choose your FUN RIDE

SPORTSTER

SUPER-10 LIGHTWEIGHT

TOPPER

DUO-GLIDE

from Harley-Davidson's "all-round" line for '60

DUO-GLIDE — Harley-Davidson's finest is the luxury cruiser of motorcycles. Smoothest ride on two wheels. Newly styled and engineered for 1960. Available in the FL series or super-powered FLH models.

SPORTSTERS — H Model (shown) for highways or byways — rough going or smooth. Also Sportster CH for "driving" through the rough in "off-the-road" competition.

NEW SUPER-10 LIGHTWEIGHT — Harley-Davidson's newest wheels for the young and young at heart. Ideal for work, school and play. Exciting new styling. Up to 80 miles per gallon.

NEW TOPPER SCOOTER — Tops all others in beauty and performance. Fashioned in gleaming chrome and fiberglass. No

shifting or clutching with *Scootaway* drive. Low center of gravity makes for easy handling.

In '60 more than ever before, there's a Harley-Davidson for every purse... every purpose. We've added the new *Super-10* Lightweight and *Topper* Scooter. We've made the famous *Duo-Glide* and *Sportster* better than ever. See the all 'round line for '60 at your dealer's now. He'll show you how easy it is to own a Harley-Davidson with his easy-pay plans. Or mail the coupon for free, colorful folders.

HARLEY-DAVIDSON MOTOR CO.
Dept. ML, Milwaukee 1, Wisconsin

Please send me information on

☐ Duo-Glides ☐ Sportsters ☐ Super-10 ☐ Topper

Name _____ Age _____

Address _____

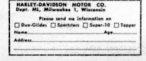

Harley-Davidson

MILWAUKEE 1, WISCONSIN

Perfect Mating of Man and Machine

14

HONDA'S POTENT TWINS

.... Sweep the West Coast in an avalanche of unsurpassable competition victories...READY TO WIN ANYWHERE, HONDA compsters grab roadracing, scrambles, cross country victories...THEN shatter all existing ECONOMY records.

LUXURIOUS STYLING has marked the CA95 (150cc) model as a beautiful yet rugged favorite. 2 cylinder, OHC, 4 cycle, this amazing 150 develops 16½ B.H.P. at 10,500 r.p.m. Incorporates (as all 125cc and 150cc models) HONDA'S famous 3-main-bearing "anti-friction" crank shaft.

$460 p.o.e.

$495 p.o.e.

RUGGED, READY FOR ACTION, (125cc) CB72 is one of HONDA'S biggest, little giants. Road-racing, scrambles or Highway touring. It's an unbeatable champ. Potent four-cycle develops 15 B.H.P. at 10,500 r.p.m.

■ 8 MODELS (all incorporate electric starters except Super Cub CA100)

ATTENTION: EAST COAST *racing enthusiasts.* *HONDA is COMING YOUR WAY!*

VISIT your local dealer and inquire when he will have *HIS FIRST* shipment of HONDA motorcycles on display. Untold scores of Eastern dealers are joining with National racing greats **EVERETT BRASHEAR** and **DICK KLAMFOTH** in America's newest and most spectacular "electric starter" motorcycle line. *REMEMBER:* 6 different models, all with 4 cycle OVER HEAD CAM engines, starting from 125cc up to 305cc...PLUS HONDA'S fabulous 2 model OVER HEAD VALVE 50cc Super Cubs...

HONDA is the WORLD'S LARGEST manufacturer of motorcycles, producing over 65,000 units EACH MONTH! AND THEY OFFER THE WORLD'S LARGEST ACCESSORY LINE TO PROVE IT!

AHM AMERICAN HONDA MOTOR CO., INC.
4077 West Pico Boulevard ● ● Los Angeles 19, California

SPECTACULAR FOR '60

The Bold and the Beautiful

New
HARLEY-DAVIDSON DUO-GLIDE

We've put this "show" on the road—the world's finest motorcycle made better than ever by the world's finest craftsmen.

Spectacular styling with gleaming new headlight nacelle of aluminum alloy. Flowing back from the nacelle, new twin-flare tank paneling adds dash to the famous Duo-Glide look. Spectacular new performance is the result of a host of new mechanical improvements . . . quieter engine, longer bearing life and faster starts.

Your Harley-Davidson dealer is *previewing* the new Duo-Glide now. He will show you the many other new features that make the Duo-Glide for '60 the greatest "road show" ever. Or mail the coupon for free, colorful folder.

Harley-Davidson
MOTOR CO.
MILWAUKEE 1, WISCONSIN
Perfect Mating of Man and Machine

HARLEY-DAVIDSON MOTOR CO.
DEPT. PS, MILWAUKEE 1, WISCONSIN

Please send me new folder on the Duo-Glide for '60

Name..Age.........

Address...

....

79

time it!

*world's
fastest
natural
tan!*

TANFASTIC

Want a honey of a tan in a hurry? There's only
one lotion with a tanning booster that gives you a faster,
natural tan... and no burning or peeling. It's Tanfastic!
And what better way to show off your Tanfastic tan
than in the swimsuit above—"Tanfastic" by White Stag!

*creamy white
available everywhere in
handy tubes or
plastic squeeze bottles!*

THE THREE BIG NEWS IN TELEVISION !

The New Look: as individual as your home, your taste, your purse. A spectrum of styles and finishes, each with General Electric's renowned picture quality. This year, there's triple the sensitivity for distant reception.

The New Sound: teaming the biggest speaker in TV, a 21 x 9-inch woofer with a high-frequency electrostatic tweeter. It's a Hi-Fi speaker system in itself, or, if you look at it this way, it can be the other half of your stereo set.

The New Control: new Four-way *Wireless* Remote Control not only turns your set on and off and changes channels, but gives you *infinite* command of volume control.

The three big TV News await you at your General Electric dealer's now. General Electric Company, Television Receiver Department, Syracuse, New York.

GENERAL ELECTRIC TV 1960 STYLE !

DANISH WALNUT richly worked in fine veneers and solids. *Two* 21 x 9-inch woofers with electrostatic tweeters. Stereo-Phono Jacks. With or without *wireless* remote. All sets shown have 262 sq. inch viewable picture area—21″ overall diagonal tube measurement.

FRENCH PROVINCIAL has two 21 x 9-inch woofers with two electrostatic tweeters. Handsomely crafted in cherry veneers and solids. Stereo-Phono Jacks. With or without Four-way *Wireless* Remote Control.

COLONIAL LO-BOY—authentic early American styling in maple veneers and hardwood solids. 6½-inch speaker. Stereo-Phono Jacks.

TVhistory.TV

  GENERAL ELECTRIC

30

COST OF LIVING 1960

The average family income in the 1960's was around $5,800. The tax rate back then was 20%, and minimum wage was $1.25/hour. The cost of a new car in the 1960's was around $2,500, but in today's values, it would be around $14,235. The price for a gallon of gas was about 31¢, which is around $2.07 today.

Movies – Going to the movies in the 1960s would set someone back $0.25. This may seem a bargain by today's standards but we need to realize that the minimum wage in 1960 was $1.25 and today it's $7.25.

Public Phones – Have you ever heard the expression "drop a dime?" That's because that was the cost of a phone call.

Stamps – First class mail cost 5 cents.

Supermarkets: A carton of eggs was $0.53, a gallon of milk was priced at $0.49 and coupons reduced the price even further. Fresh fruits and vegetables remained steady depending on the season and availability from $0.10 to $0.50 a pound. For less than $0.90, a housewife could purchase six cans of Campbell's soup. For $0.79 a one-pound of bacon could be had, but for the same price, one could purchase 2-pounds of beef chuck roast.

Fast Food – McDonald's burgers were $0.15 apiece and they had promotions in which costumers could get 10 burgers for $1.00.

Electronics were practically non-existent by today's standards but those that existed were out or reach to main stream Americans. For instance, the first microwave available to the masses was marketed by Amana and the cost of this basic 2-button microwave was in the $500 range. Most microwave ovens well into the late 60s were unaffordable conveniences that only a few thousand people owned.

For those who lived through the 1960s as young adults, the biggest component of any bachelor pad included a stereo system with "high-fidelity" speakers. The prices were exorbitant for basic bookshelf speakers and reaching into the thousands of dollars for space-hugging floor to ceiling speakers.

By comparison, electronics have become more powerful, miniaturized and mostly affordable. The quality of the products has increased as well and so has the storage capacity of computers and handheld devices.

When it came to portable music, a small $200 dollar transistor radio was the most basic and "affordable" choice. The perks included portability, exclusively AM stations and one speaker for mono-sound. Recorded music consisted of vinyl record albums played in the standard, and expensive, two-speaker home stereo system.

Television sets were heavy things that dominated the family's living room much as they did in the late 1950s. CRT television sets in color were available but expensive to own. Programming was not as varied as it is today and people spent more time socializing than watching TV.

The average cost of a television set was less than $300 but this was a huge expense for people earning under $6,000 a year. Reception was spotty in some locations and weather factors would completely eliminate transmission. Manually adjusting the indoor antenna or climbing on the roof to restore picture to the set was very common.

A list of goods in 1960

Oxford Men's shoes	**$12.95**
Oranges: 2 dozen	89 cents
Oven ready Turkeys	**39 cents per pound**
A Gallon of Milk	49 cents
1 Dozen Eggs	**53 cents**
One regular size bottle of Heinz ketchup	22 cents
One-ounce Hershey bar	**5 cents**
Pound of pork chops	$1.03
Pound of sirloin steak	**85 cents**
Six-pack of Pepsi	59 cents
Can of shaving cream	**59 cents**
Can of hair spray	47 cents
Six-pack of beer	**99 cents**
Loaf of Bread	20 cents
Fast Food Hamburger	**15 cents**
Frozen French Fried Potatoes	10 cents for 8 ounces
Gerber's Baby Food	**25 cents for 3**
Ice Cream	79 cents half gallon
Jello	**35 cents for 4 packs**
Kraft Miracle Whip	51 cents
Skippy Peanut Butter	**79 cents**
Sugar	38 cents for 5 pounds
Toothpaste Crest	**50 cents**
Watermelon	2½ cents per pound
Bacon	**79 cents per pound**

F. W. Woolworth Co.

BACON and TOMATO..........45c *Toasted Three Decker Sandwich*	**PLAIN or TOASTED SANDWICHES**
BAKED HAM and CHEESE........50c *Toasted Three Decker Sandwich*	**BAKED HAM Sandwich**..........30c
CHICKEN SALAD ....55c *Toasted Three Decker Sandwich*	**HAM SALAD Sandwich**..........25c
HAM SALAD and EGG SALAD.....45c *Toasted Three Decker Sandwich*	**EGG SALAD Sandwich**..........25c
	AMERICAN CHEESE Sandwich.....25c

Fountain Features

DE LUXE **TULIP SUNDAE 25c** 2 Dippers of Ice Cream covered with Crushed Fruit or Fresh Fruits in Season CHOICE OF STRAWBERRY, PINEAPPLE, CHERRY, CHOCOLATE OR HOT FUDGE Topped with Whipped Topping Roasted Nuts and Cherry Ring	SUPER JUMBO **BANANA SPLIT 39c** ½ Banana covered with 3 Dippers of Ice Cream and Crushed Fruits or Fresh Fruits in Season CHOICE OF STRAWBERRY, PINEAPPLE, CHERRY, CHOCOLATE OR HOT FUDGE Topped with Whipped Topping and Roasted Nuts	**EXTRA RICH** **ICE CREAM SODA 25c** POPULAR FLAVORS Made with 2 Dippers of Ice Cream Crushed Fruit or Fresh Fruits in Season

MALTED MILK 25c
Popular FLAVORS   Made with 2 Dippers of Ice Cream

MILK SHAKE 25c
Popular FLAVORS   Made with 2 Dippers of Ice Cream

BANANA SPLIT Regular 25c
Popular FLAVORS   Made with 3 Dippers of Ice Cream

FRESH ORANGE JUICE......... Regular 20c Large 30c
Freshly Squeezed to Order

Cooling Drinks

FRESH FRUIT LEMONADE.............10¢

WOOLWORTH'S ORANGE DRINK Large ..10¢

ICED TEA WITH LEMON WEDGE.......10¢

Home Style Desserts

APPLE PIE....................Per Cut 15¢
5¢ Additional with Ice Cream

LAYER CAKE..................Per Cut 15¢
5¢ Additional with Ice Cream

WOOLWORTH COFFEE—ALWAYS GOOD

HAVE A COKE   GOES GOOD WITH FOOD

PRINTED IN U.S.A.   NO. 3454 REV. 4-60

1960 Woolworth menu

FAMOUS BIRTHS

Gregory Efthimios Louganis was born January 29, 1960 is an American Olympic diver, LGBT activist, and author who won gold medals at the 1984 and 1988 Summer Olympics, on both the springboard and platform. Greg Louganis was born in El Cajon, California, and is of Samoan and Swedish descent. He is the only male and the second diver in Olympic history to sweep the diving events in consecutive Olympic Games. He has been called both "the greatest American diver" and "probably the greatest diver in history". At the 1988 Seoul Olympics, his head struck the springboard during the preliminary rounds, leading to a concussion. He completed the preliminaries despite his injury. He then earned the highest single score of the qualifying round for his next dive and repeated the dive during the finals, earning the gold medal by a margin of 25 points. In the 10 m finals, he won the gold medal, performing a 3.4 difficulty dive in his last attempt, earning 86.70 points for a total of 638.61, surpassing silver medalist Xiong Ni by only 1.14 points.

Robert Smigel was born February 7, 1960 is an American actor, humorist, puppeteer, comedian and writer. Robert grew up in New York City and first established himself as a writer on Saturday Night Live. In 1996, Smigel wrote and performed on the short-lived Dana Carvey Show, a primetime sketch comedy program on ABC. Despite its premature end, the show provided Smigel the opportunity to debut his first cartoon, The Ambiguously Gay Duo. Smigel's most famous creation, however, would be the foul-mouthed puppet Triumph the Insult Comic Dog, who mercilessly mocks celebrities and others in the style of a Borscht Belt comedian. This character debuted on Late Night with Conan O'Brien in February 1997 and would continue to make appearances on the show. It was reported in 2006 that Smigel and Adam Sandler were working on an animated sitcom for Fox called Animals. Fox has not made any official statement regarding the show. He co-wrote and co-executive produced the films Hotel Transylvania and Hotel Transylvania 2, in which he voiced Marty.

Robert Patrick Casey Jr. was born April 13, 1960. He is an American attorney and politician serving as the senior United States Senator from Pennsylvania, a seat to which he was first elected in 2006. Born in Scranton, Pennsylvania, Robert Casey is the son of Bob Casey, a former Governor of Pennsylvania. In 2002, Casey attempted to follow in his father's footsteps by running for Governor of Pennsylvania, but was defeated in the Democratic primary by eventual general election victor Ed Rendell. After being term-limited out of his position as Auditor General, Casey was elected Treasurer in the 2004 election. Casey defeated two-term Republican incumbent Rick Santorum in the 2006 United States Senate election in Pennsylvania. He was reelected in 2012, becoming the first Democrat to win re-election to the U.S. Senate from Pennsylvania since Joseph S. Clark Jr. in 1962. In 2018, Casey defeated Republican U.S. Representative Lou Barletta to win a third term.

Jaron Zepel Lanier was born May 3, 1960. He is an American computer philosophy writer, computer scientist, visual artist, and composer of classical music. Considered a founding father of the field of virtual reality, Lanier and Thomas G. Zimmerman left Atari in 1985 to found VPL Research, Inc., the first company to sell VR goggles and gloves. In the late 1990s, Lanier worked on applications for Internet2, and in the 2000s, he was a visiting scholar at Silicon Graphics and various universities. In 2006 he began to work at Microsoft, and from 2009 has worked at Microsoft Research as an Interdisciplinary Scientist. Lanier has composed classical music and is a collector of rare instruments; his acoustic album, Instruments of Change (1994) features Asian wind and string instruments such as the khene mouth organ, the suling flute, and the sitar-like esraj. Lanier teamed with Mario Grigorov to compose the soundtrack to the documentary film, The Third Wave (2007). In 2010, Lanier was nominated in the TIME 100 list of most influential people.

John Conant Flansburgh was born May 6, 1960 and is an American musician. John Flansburgh was born in Lincoln, Massachusetts. He is half of the long-standing Brooklyn, New York-based alternative rock duo They Might Be Giants, for which he writes, sings, and plays rhythm guitar. Commonly referred to by the nickname Flans or Flansy, he is married to musician Robin Goldwasser, with whom he occasionally performs. John Flansburgh co-founded They Might Be Giants, with longtime friend John Linnell, in 1982 while a student at Pratt Institute. The two share singing and songwriting duties, with Flansburgh on guitar, in addition to performing a variety of instruments when the need arises. In the 2002 documentary Gigantic: A Tale of Two Johns, he was described as holding a leadership role in the group, managing most details of their live act and handling much of the promotion effort. Flansburgh has pursued a number of solo projects during his time with They Might Be Giants. His band Mono Puff recorded two full-length albums in the late 1990s and toured occasionally.

Steven Siro Vai was born June 6, 1960 and is an American guitarist, composer, singer, songwriter, and producer. A three-time Grammy Award winner and fifteen-time nominee, Vai started his music career in 1978 at the age of eighteen as a transcriptionist for Frank Zappa, and played in Zappa's band from 1980 to 1983. He embarked on a solo career in 1983 and has released eight solo albums to date. He has recorded and toured with Alcatrazz, David Lee Roth, and Whitesnake, as well as recording with artists such as Public Image Ltd, Mary J. Blige, Spinal Tap, and Ozzy Osbourne. Additionally, Vai has toured with live-only acts G3, Zappa Plays Zappa, and the Experience Hendrix tour, as well as headlining international tours.

He released his first solo album Flex-Able in 1984, while his most successful release, Passion and Warfare (1990), was described as "the richest and best hard rock guitar-virtuoso album of the '80s".

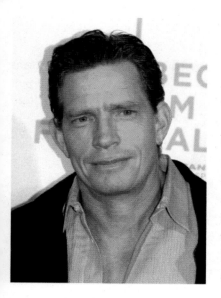

Thomas Haden Church born June 17, 1960 and is an American actor, director, and writer. Thomas Church was born as Thomas Richard McMillen in Woodland, Yolo County, California. Church started in the entertainment business as a radio personality and doing voice-over work. He worked in television for two more seasons with a lead role on Ned & Stacey opposite Debra Messing. He has had supporting roles in films such as Tombstone, George of the Jungle, and The Specials. He has often played villains or comic relief in films, such as in Demon Knight. He has since appeared in films such as Idiocrasy, done voice-over work on films such as Over the Hedge and starred in one of AMC's highest rated television productions, Broken Trail, with Robert Duvall, in 2006, for which he won an Emmy. In 2007, he appeared as the tragic villain Sandman in Sam Raimi's Spider-Man 3 starring Tobey Maguire and Kirsten Dunst. In 2005, he was invited to join the Academy of Motion Picture Arts and Sciences.

Erin Brockovich was born June 22, 1960 she is an American legal clerk, consumer advocate, and environmental activist, who, despite her lack of formal education in the law, was instrumental in building a case against the Pacific Gas and Electric Company (PG&E) of California in 1993. Erin Brockovich was born Erin Pattee in Lawrence, Kansas. Her successful lawsuit was the subject of a 2000 film, Erin Brockovich, which starred Julia Roberts. Since then, Brockovich has become a media personality as well, hosting the TV series Challenge America with Erin Brockovich on ABC and Final Justice on Zone Reality. She is the president of Brockovich Research & Consulting. She also works as a consultant for Girardi & Keese, the New York law firm of Weitz & Luxenberg, which has a focus on personal injury claims for asbestos exposure, and Shine Lawyers in Australia. In 2003, Brockovich received settlements of $430,000 from two parties and an undisclosed amount from a third party to settle her lawsuit alleging toxic mold in her Agoura Hills, California, home.

Deborah Christine "Siedah" Garrett was born June 24, 1960 is an American singer and songwriter, who has written songs and performed backing vocals for many recording artists in the music industry, such as Michael Jackson, The Pointer Sisters, Brand New Heavies, Quincy Jones, Tevin Campbell, Donna Summer, Madonna, Jennifer Hudson among others. Garrett was born in Los Angeles and raised in Compton, where she started singing as a child. In 1987 Garrett was involved in Michael Jackson's Bad album, singing a duet with Jackson on "I Just Can't Stop Loving You" in several different languages. She co-wrote Jackson's No. 1 single "Man in the Mirror". In a 2013 interview with Luka Neskovic, Garrett said: "All I wanted to do was give Michael something he would want to say to the world, and I knew it couldn't be another 'Oh baby, I love you' song. In 2006, Garrett contributed her songwriting services to Bill Condon's film adaptation of Dreamgirls, providing lyrics for two of the four new songs added to the score.

David William Duchovny was born August 7, 1960 and is an American actor, writer, producer, director, novelist, and singer-songwriter. He is known for playing FBI agent Fox Mulder on the television series The X-Files and writer Hank Moody on the television series Californication, both of which have earned him Golden Globe awards. David Duchovny appeared in both X-Files films, the 1998 science fiction-thriller of the same name and the supernatural-thriller The X-Files: I Want to Believe (2008). He executive-produced and starred in the historically based cop drama Aquarius (2015–16). Duchovny earned a A.B. in English literature from Princeton University, and an M.A. in English literature from Yale University, and has since published three books, Holy Cow: A Modern-Day Dairy Tale (2015), Bucky F*cking Dent (2016) and Miss Subways (2018). He appeared in a celebrity edition of Who Wants to Be a Millionaire? in May 2000. He got to the $250,000 question, but answered his $500,000 question incorrectly and lost $218,000, leaving him with $32,000.

Sean Justin Penn was born August 17, 1960 is an American actor, director and filmmaker. Penn began his acting career in television, with a brief appearance in Little House on the Prairie, December 4, 1974, and directed by his father Leo Penn. He became known as a prominent leading actor with the drama Dead Man Walking (1995), for which he earned his first Academy Award nomination and the Best Actor Award at the Berlin Film Festival. Sean Penn received another two Oscar nominations for Woody Allen's comedy-drama Sweet and Lowdown (1999) and the drama I Am Sam, before winning his first Academy Award for Best Actor in 2003 for Mystic River and a second one in 2008 for Milk. Sean Penn made his feature film directorial debut with The Indian Runner, followed by the drama film The Crossing Guard and the mystery film The Pledge. Penn directed one of the 11 segments of 11'09"01 September 11, a compilation film made in response to the September 11 attacks. His fourth feature film, the biographical drama survival movie Into the Wild, garnered critical acclaim and two Academy Award nominations.

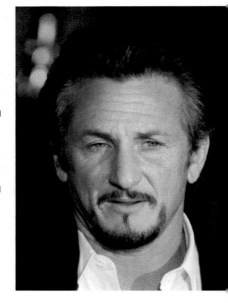

Daryl Christine Hannah was born December 3, 1960 and is an American actress and environmental activist. Hannah was born in Chicago, Illinois. Hannah made her film debut in 1978 with an appearance in Brian De Palma's horror film The Fury. In 1982, Hannah played the acrobatic and violent replicant Pris in Ridley Scott's science fiction classic Blade Runner, in which she performed some of her own gymnastic stunts. That same year she appeared in the summer hit release Summer Lovers. She then was cast as a mermaid in Ron Howard's 1984 fantasy Splash, which starred Tom Hanks. Hannah played the daughter of Jack Lemmon's character in both of the Grumpy Old Men comedies. That same year, she played Nancy Archer in the HBO comedy remake of Attack Of The Fifty-Foot Woman. In the early 2000s, her most memorable role may be that of the one-eyed assassin, Elle Driver, in Kill Bill. Since 2015, she has appeared in Sense8, a series on Netflix from the Wachowskis. The series ran for two seasons, with a finale episode released on June 8, 2018.

SPORTING EVENTS 1960

NFL 1960 Championship Game

Green bay Packers

13

Philadelphia Eagles

17

The 1960 National Football League championship game was the 28th NFL title game. The game was played on Monday, December 26, at Franklin Field in Philadelphia, Pennsylvania.

The game matched the league's conference champions, Philadelphia Eagles (10–2) of the East and Green Bay Packers (8–4) of the West. The Eagles were making their first appearance in a championship game since 1949 and the Packers their first since 1944. Two years earlier, both teams had finished last in their respective conferences. Due to the lack of lights at Franklin Field, the kickoff time was moved up to 12 p.m. (noon) EST. The league was concerned about the possibility of sudden death overtime, as had occurred in 1958. The game was played on a Monday, similar to 1955, as the NFL did not want to play on Christmas.

A capacity crowd of 67,325 gathered at Franklin Field, the home field of the University of Pennsylvania, with 7,000 temporary seats having been added. The Eagles were a two to three-point home underdog, and the game-time temperature was 48 °F (9 °C), creating difficult inconsistent field conditions for both teams, as the frozen playing surface thawed in spots leaving scattered puddles under the low winter sun.

The 1960 game represented a chance for Philadelphia to add to the consecutive titles they won in 1948 and 1949, but the team had declined to only two wins in 1958. Head coach Buck Shaw was in his third season with the Eagles, and in what turned out to be his final year as a head coach, and had turned around the team from a 2–9–1 record in 1958 to seven wins in 1959 to a conference championship and the league's best record in 1960. The Eagles were led on the field by 34-year-old quarterback Norm Van Brocklin, who was ranked second in the NFL with 2,471 passing yards and 24 passing touchdowns, behind Unitas of the Colts in both statistics, and was playing in his final game. Less than a month after the title game, he was named the head coach of the expansion Minnesota Vikings. Philadelphia had clinched the Eastern title early on December 4 at 9–1, and there was concern by Shaw that it could have an adverse effect on his team.

1960 World Series

Pittsburgh Pirates

4

New York Yankees

3

The 1960 World Series was played between the Pittsburgh Pirates of the National League (NL) and the New York Yankees of the American League (AL) from October 5–13, 1960. In Game 7, Bill Mazeroski hit a walk-off ninth-inning home run, the first time a winner-take-all World Series game ended with a walk-off home run.

Despite losing the series, the Yankees scored 55 runs, the most runs scored by any one team in World Series history, and more than twice as many as the Pirates, who scored 27. The Yankees won three blowouts (16–3, 10–0, and 12–0), while the Pirates won four close games (6–4, 3–2, 5–2, and 10–9) to win the series. The Series MVP was Bobby Richardson of the Yankees, the only time in history that the award has been given to a member of the losing team.

Game	Date	Score	Location	Time	Attendance
1	October 5	New York Yankees – 4, **Pittsburgh Pirates** – 6	Forbes Field	2:29	36,676
2	October 6	**New York Yankees** – 16, Pittsburgh Pirates – 3	Forbes Field	3:14	37,308
3	October 8	Pittsburgh Pirates – 0, **New York Yankees** – 10	Yankee Stadium	2:41	70,001
4	October 9	**Pittsburgh Pirates** – 3, New York Yankees – 2	Yankee Stadium	2:29	67,812
5	October 10	**Pittsburgh Pirates** – 5, New York Yankees – 2	Yankee Stadium	2:32	62,753
6	October 12	**New York Yankees** – 12, Pittsburgh Pirates – 0	Forbes Field	2:38	38,580
7	October 13	New York Yankees – 9, **Pittsburgh Pirates** – 10	Forbes Field	2:36	36,683

1960 NBA Finals

ST. LOUIS HAWKS
St. Louis Hawks

3

Boston Celtics

4

The 1960 NBA World Championship Series was the championship series of the 1960 NBA Playoffs, which concluded the National Basketball Association 1959–60 season. The best-of-seven series was played between the Western Conference champion St. Louis Hawks and the Eastern Conference champion Boston Celtics. It was Boston's fourth trip to the NBA Finals and St. Louis' third. The Celtics beat the Hawks 4–3. The Finals featured Hall of Famers Bill Russell, Bob Cousy, Tom Heinsohn, Frank Ramsey, Sam Jones, K.C. Jones, Coach Red Auerbach, Bob Pettit, Cliff Hagan, Slater Martin, Clyde Lovellette, and Coach Alex Hannum.

This was the last time the NBA Finals would be played in March.

Game	Date	Home Team	Score	Road Team
Game 1 at Boston.	Sun. March 27	**Boston Celtics**	140–122 (1–0)	St. Louis Hawks
Game 2 at Boston	Tue. March 29	Boston Celtics	103–113 (1–1)	**St. Louis Hawks**
Game 3 at St. Louis.	Sat. April 2	St. Louis Hawks	86–102 (1–2)	**Boston Celtics**
Game 4 at St. Louis	Sun. April 3	**St. Louis Hawks**	106–96 (2–2)	Boston Celtics
Game 5 at Boston.	Tue. April 5	**Boston Celtics**	127–102 (3–2)	St. Louis Hawks
Game 6 at St. Louis.	Thu. April 7	**St. Louis Hawks**	105–102 (3–3)	Boston Celtics
Game 7 at Boston	Sat. April 9	**Boston Celtics**	122–103 (4–3)	St. Louis Hawks

1960 Stanley Cup Winners

Montreal Canadiens	Toronto Maple Leafs
4	0

The 1959–60 NHL season was the 43rd season of the National Hockey League. The Montreal Canadiens were the Stanley Cup winners as they defeated the Toronto Maple Leafs four games to none for their fifth straight Stanley Cup.

Montreal played the minimum number of games to win the Stanley Cup and in the process, became the last Cup winners in NHL history to go undefeated in the playoffs to date. After winning the Stanley Cup, Maurice Richard retired from the NHL as a champion.

Doug Harvey wins the James Norris Memorial Trophy and Jacques Plante wins Vezina Trophy

Toronto Maple Leafs	2–4	Montreal Canadiens
Toronto Maple Leafs	1–2	Montreal Canadiens
Montreal Canadiens	5–2	Toronto Maple Leafs
Montreal Canadiens	4–0	Toronto Maple Leafs

Montreal won series 4–0

1960 US Open Golf

The 1960 U.S. Open was the 60th U.S. Open, held June 16–18 at Cherry Hills Country Club in Englewood, Colorado, a suburb of Denver. Arnold Palmer staged the greatest comeback in U.S. Open history, erasing a seven-stroke deficit during the final round to win his only U.S. Open title. It is remembered as a crossroads for the three primary contenders in the final round: Palmer, Ben Hogan, and amateur Jack Nicklaus, three of the greatest players in the history of golf.

Having already won the Masters, Arnold Palmer was half-way to the single-season Grand Slam with his win at Cherry Hills. His quest ended three weeks later at the British Open, when he lost to Kel Nagle by one stroke at St Andrews. Two weeks later, he finished five strokes back in a tie for seventh at the PGA Championship, the only major that eluded him for his career. This was Palmer's only victory at the U.S. Open; he finished second four times, including three losses in playoffs in 1962, 1963, and 1966.

This was the third major championship at Cherry Hills, which previously hosted the U.S. Open in 1938 and the PGA Championship in 1941. The U.S. Open returned in 1978 and the PGA Championship in 1985. The average elevation of the course exceeds 5,300 feet (1,620 m) above sea level.

Place	Player	Country	Score	To par	Money ($)
1	**Arnold Palmer**	United States	72-71-72-65=280	−4	14,400
2	Jack Nicklaus (a)	United States	71-71-69-71=282	−2	0
T3	Julius Boros	United States	73-69-68-73=283	−1	3,950
	Dow Finsterwald	United States	71-69-70-73=283		
	Jack Fleck	United States	70-70-72-71=283		
	Dutch Harrison	United States	74-70-70-69=283		
	Ted Kroll	United States	72-69-75-67=283		
	Mike Souchak	United States	68-67-73-75=283		
T9	Don Cherry (a)	United States	70-71-71-72=284	E	0
	Jerry Barber	United States	69-71-70-74=284		1,950
	Ben Hogan	United States	75-67-69-73=284		

Arnold Palmer trailed leader Mike Souchak by eight strokes after 36 holes and by seven shots after 54 holes. Almost everyone believed he was out of contention beginning the final round, tied for fifteenth place. Palmer drove the green on the par-4 1st to set up a two-putt birdie, and then chipped in from 90 feet (27 m) for birdie at the second. After nearly making an eagle at 3 and tapping in for another birdie, he holed an 18-footer for birdie at 4 then made two more birdies at 6 and 7. He cooled off the rest of his round, finally carding a 65 (−6) for a 280 (−4) total. It was the second lowest final round in U.S. Open history, behind only Johnny Miller's 63 in the final round of the 1973 U.S. Open at Oakmont Country Club.

Twenty-year-old Jack Nicklaus, the reigning U.S. Amateur champion playing in his fourth Open, was also in contention during the final round, briefly holding the lead after making eagle at 5 and birdie at 9. Two three-putts on the back-nine dropped him to a 282 (−2) total, two strokes behind Palmer.

1960 Kentucky Derby

The 1960 Kentucky Derby was the 86th running of the Kentucky Derby. The race took place on May 7, 1960.

Finished	Post	Horse	Jockey	Trainer	Owner	Time
1st	7	Venetian Way	Bill Hartack	Victor J. Sovinski	Sunny Blue Farm (Isaac Blumberg)	2:02 2/5
2nd	2	Bally Ache	Bobby Ussery	Jimmy Pitt	Edgehill Farm	
3rd	9	Victoria Park	Manuel Ycaza	Horatio Luro	Windfields Farm	

1960 Preakness Stakes

The 1960 Preakness Stakes was the 85th running of the $175,000 Preakness Stakes thoroughbred horse race. The race took place on May 21, 1960, and was televised in the United States on the CBS television network. Bally Ache, who was jockeyed by Robert Ussery, won the race by four lengths over runner-up Victoria Park. Approximate post time was 5:48 p.m. Eastern Time. The race was run on a fast track in a final time of 1:57-3/5 The Maryland Jockey Club reported total attendance of 30,659, this is recorded as second highest on the list of American thoroughbred racing top attended events for North America in 1960.

Finish Position	Margin (lengths)	Post Position	Horse name	Jockey	Trainer	Owner
1st	0	1	Bally Ache	Robert Ussery	Jimmy Pitt	Edgehill Farm
2nd	4	4	Victoria Park	Anthony DeSpirito	Horatio Luro	Windfields Farm
3rd	53/4	3	Celtic Ash	Sam Boulmetis	Thomas J. Barry	Green Dunes Farm

1960 Belmont Stakes

The day prior to the Belmont Stakes, betting favorite Bally Ache came up lame and was withdrawn from the 1¼ mile third leg of the Triple Crown. His absence left Venetian Way ridden by Eddie Arcaro, as the favorite. However, winning the Belmont Stakes with an underdog was nothing new for Celtic Ash's owner, Joseph O'Connell. Two years earlier in 1958, he and trainer Tom Barry won the Classic with the lightly raced Irish-bred colt Cavan. On June 11, 1960, O'Connell was in a Brighton, Massachusetts, hospital and watched on television as Hartack brought his colt from last place to overtake Venetian Way in the stretch, then pull away to win easily by five and a half lengths.

The Triple Crown

The Triple Crown of Thoroughbred Racing, commonly known as the Triple Crown, is a title awarded to a three-year-old Thoroughbred horse who wins the Kentucky Derby, Preakness Stakes, and Belmont Stakes. The three races were inaugurated in different years, the last being the Kentucky Derby in 1875. These races are now run annually in May and early June of each year. The Triple Crown Trophy, commissioned in 1950 but awarded to all previous winners as well as those after 1950, is awarded to a Triple Crown winner.

1960 Boxing

Muhammad Ali born Cassius Marcellus Clay Jr. on January 17, 1942 and passed away June 3, 2016. He was an American professional boxer, activist, and philanthropist. Nicknamed "The Greatest," he is widely regarded as one of the most significant and celebrated sports figures of the 20th century and as one of the greatest boxers of all time. Ali was born and raised in Louisville, Kentucky, and began training as an amateur boxer at age 12. At 18, he won a gold medal in the light heavyweight division at the 1960 Summer Olympics, and turned professional later that year. He converted to Islam and became a Muslim after 1961, and eventually took the name Muhammad Ali. Ali was a leading heavyweight boxer of the 20th century, and he remains the only three-time lineal champion of that division. His joint records of beating 21 boxers for the world heavyweight title and winning 14 unified title bouts stood for 35 years.

Floyd Patterson Regains Heavyweight Championship

Floyd Patterson knocked out Johansson in the fifth round of their rematch on June 20, 1960, to become the first man in history to regain the Undisputed World Heavyweight Championship. Johansson hit the canvas hard, seemingly out before he landed flat on his back. With glazed eyes, blood trickling from his mouth and his left foot quivering, he was counted out. Johansson lay unconscious for five minutes before he was helped onto a stool.

A third fight between them was held on March 13, 1961 and while Johansson put Patterson on the floor, Patterson retained his title by knockout in the sixth round to win the rubber match in which Patterson was decked twice and Johansson, once in the first round. Johansson had landed both right hands over Floyd's left jab. After getting up from the second knockdown, Floyd abandoned his jab and connected with a left hook that knocked down Johansson. After that, Patterson came on with a strong body attack that wore down Johansson. In the 6th round, Johansson caught Patterson with a solid right. But the power in Ingemar's punches was gone. Patterson won the fight in the 6th round by knockout.

1960 Winter Olympics

The 1960 Winter Olympics, officially known as the VIII Olympic Winter Games, was a winter multi-sport event held between February 18–28, 1960 in Squaw Valley, California, United States.

Squaw Valley was chosen to host the Games at the 1956 meeting of the International Olympic Committee (IOC). It was an undeveloped resort in 1955, so from 1956 to 1960 the infrastructure and all of the venues were built at a cost of US$80,000,000. It was designed to be intimate, allowing spectators and competitors to walk to nearly all the venues. Squaw Valley hosted athletes from thirty nations who competed in four sports and twenty-seven events. Women's speed skating and biathlon made their Olympic debuts. The organizers decided the bobsled events did not warrant the cost to build a venue, so for the first and only time bobsled was not on the Winter Olympic program.

Rank	Nation	Gold	Silver	Bronze	Total
1	Soviet Union	7	5	9	21
2	United Team of Germany	4	3	1	8
3	United States*	3	4	3	10
4	Norway	3	3	0	6
5	Sweden	3	2	2	7
6	Finland	2	3	3	8
7	Canada	2	1	1	4
8	Switzerland	2	0	0	2
9	Austria	1	2	3	6
10	France	1	0	2	3
11	Netherlands	0	1	1	2
11	Poland	0	1	1	2
13	Czechoslovakia	0	1	0	1
14	Italy	0	0	1	1
Totals (14 nations)		28	26	27	81

* With blue background denotes home nation

Athletes from 30 nations competed at the 1960 Games. South Africa competed at the Winter Games for the first time; it would be the last for many years, as apartheid policies prevented South African participation until 1994. Athletes from West Germany (FRG) and East Germany (GDR) competed together as the United Team of Germany from 1956 to 1964.

BOOKS PUBLISHED IN 1960

The High Crusade is a science fiction novel by American writer Poul Anderson, about the consequences of an extraterrestrial scout ship landing in Medieval England. Poul Anderson described the novel as "one of the most popular things I've ever done, going through many book editions in several languages."

The High Crusade was originally serialized in the July–August–September 1960 issues of Astounding.

First published in book form in 1960 by Doubleday, it has been published in (at least) June 1964 and September 1968 (by Macfadden Books), 1983, 1991 (by the SFBC and again by Baen Books), 2003, and most recently in 2010. It is in print with a paperback edition issued by Baen Books in 2010 with ISBN 978-1-4391-3377-4.

Anderson's work was nominated for a Hugo Award in 1961, and was adapted into a 1983 wargame The High Crusade of the same name by TSR, Inc. and into a motion picture of the same name in 1994. Poul Anderson wrote one sequel short story, "Quest", which originally appeared in Ares magazine in the same issue that saw the original publication of the wargame

A Kind of Loving is a novel by the English novelist Stan Barstow. It has also been translated into a film of the same name, a television series, a radio play and a stage play. A Kind of Loving was the first of a trilogy, published over the course of sixteen years that followed hero Vic Brown through marriage, divorce and a move from the mining town of Cressley to London. The other two parts are The Watchers on the Shore and The Right True End. The story presents us to Vic Brown, a young working class man from Yorkshire, England, who is slowly inching his way up from his working-class roots through a white-collar job. Vic finds himself trapped by the frightening reality of his girlfriend Ingrid's pregnancy and is forced into marrying her and moving in with his mother-in-law due to a housing shortage in their Northern England town. The story is about love and loneliness. Vic meets and is very attracted to the beautiful but demanding Ingrid. As their relationship develops and transforms into real-life everyday aridity and boredom, Vic ultimately comes to terms with his life and what it really means to love. The novel has had some influence on the literary community, leaving the label "lad-lit" behind, although the term itself was not coined until the 1990s.

Clea, published in 1960, is the fourth volume in The Alexandria Quartet series by British author Lawrence Durrell. Set in Alexandria, Egypt, around World War II, the first three volumes tell the same story from different points of view, and Clea relates subsequent events.

The book begins with the Narrator (Darley) living on a remote Greek island with Nessim's illegitimate daughter from Melissa. The child is now six years old. Darley has been able to spend this period on the island—thinking, writing, maturing—due to the £500 left him in his will by the writer. Mnemjian arrives to see Darley with a message from Nessim and news of events in Alexandria—notably the fall from prosperity of the Hosnani family. Mnemjian is a prosperous barber, and possibly brothel owner.

They proceed to Alexandria, now under nightly bombardment because of the War (WW2), Darley continues to reminisce, sometimes lamenting, and seeks and sometimes finds, the characters of the earlier book.
He runs into Clea in the street - and they effortlessly pick up an affaire de coeur - this time unencumbered by the interfering physical presences of Justine and Melissa.

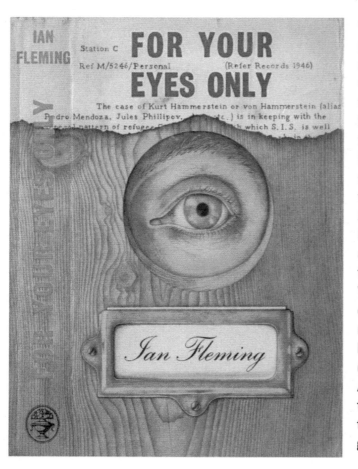

"For Your Eyes Only" begins with the murder of the Havelocks, a British couple in Jamaica who have refused to sell their estate to Herr von Hammerstein, a former Gestapo officer who is the chief of counterintelligence for the Cuban secret service. They are killed by two Cuban hitmen at the direction of their leader, Major Gonzales; all three work for von Hammerstein. The Havelocks turn out to be close friends of M, who served as the groom's best man during their wedding in 1925. M subsequently gives Bond a voluntary assignment, unconnected to sanctioned Secret Service duties, to travel to Vermont via Canada, find von Hammerstein at his rented estate at Echo Lake and assassinate him as a warning to future criminals who might think to target British citizens.
When Bond arrives on the scene, he finds the Havelocks' daughter, Judy, who intends to carry out her own mission o revenge with a bow and arrow. Judy kills von Hammerstein by shooting him in the back with an arrow from 100 yards (91 m) away at the exact moment that he dives into a lake. A shoot-out then occurs between Bond and Gonzales and the two Cuban gunmen. Bond kills all of them and returns to Canada with Judy, who has been wounded during the gunfight.

The Weirdstone of Brisingamen: A Tale of Alderley is a children's fantasy novel written by the English author Alan Garner (born 1934). Garner began work on the novel, his literary debut, in 1957 after he moved into the late medieval house Toad Hall, in Blackden, Cheshire.

The story, which took the local legend of The Wizard of the Edge as a partial basis for the novel's plot, was influenced by the folklore and landscape of the neighboring Alderley Edge where he had grown up. Upon completion the book was picked up by the publisher Sir William Collins who released it through his publishing company Collins in 1960.

The novel, set in and around Macclesfield and Alderley Edge in Cheshire, tells the story of two children, Colin and Susan, who are staying with some old friends of their mother while their parents are overseas. Susan possesses a small tear-shaped jewel held in a bracelet: unknown to her, this is the weirdstone of the title. Its nature is revealed when the children are hunted by the minions of the dark spirit Nastrond who, centuries before, had been defeated and banished by a powerful king.

The children also have to compete with the wicked shape-shifting sorceress Selina Place and the evil wizard Grimnir, each of whom wishes to possess the weirdstone. Along the way Colin and Susan are aided by the wizard Cadellin Silverbrow and his dwarf companions.

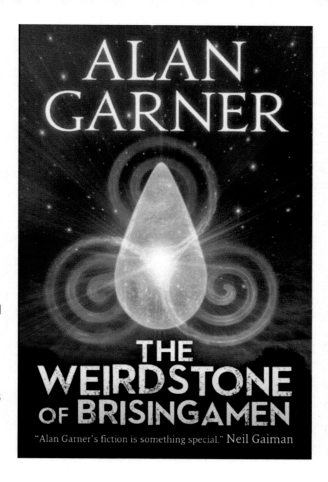

ALAN GARNER

THE WEIRDSTONE OF BRISINGAMEN

"Alan Garner's fiction is something special." Neil Gaiman

The BALLAD of PECKHAM RYE

Muriel Spark

The Ballad of Peckham Rye is a novel written in 1960 by the Scottish author Muriel Spark.

It tells the story of a devilish Scottish migrant, Dougal Douglas, who moves to Peckham in London and wreaks havoc amongst the lives of the inhabitants. The text draws upon the supernatural, as well as issues of Irish and Scottish migrancy and offers a critique of the sterile and unremarkable nature of the lives of the Peckham working class.

The novel begins with the telling of Humphrey Place saying "No" at the altar where he was due to marry Dixie Morse. Humphrey's immoral behavior is assumed to be a result of his recent association with Dougal Douglas, a Scottish migrant who has since left the area of Peckham. Spark goes on to tell us the entire story of what exactly happened during Dougal's residence in Peckham. From his inaugural meeting with Mr. V. R. Druce, head of nylon textiles manufacturers Meadows, Meade & Grindley, we learn that Dougal is employed to bridge the gap between industry and the arts. He befriends employees Merle Coverdale and Elaine Kent, an "experienced controller of process", as well as Humphrey Place, a refrigerator engineer. After finding lodgings with Miss Belle Frierne and splitting up with his fiancé Jinny due to her being ill, Dougal embarks upon a mission of disruption throughout Peckham. Throughout this he falls foul of typist Dixie Morse and electrician Trevor Lomas and becomes the target of a gang consisting of Trevor, Collie Gould and Lesley Crewe.

Border Country is a novel by Raymond Williams. The book was re-published in December 2005 as one of the first group of titles in the Library of Wales series, having been out of print for several years. Written in English, the novel was first published in 1960.

It is set in rural South Wales, close to the border with England, as demarcated by Offa's Dyke. An academic visits his sick father, who was a railway signalman. There are lengthy flashbacks to the 1920s and 1930s, including the 1926 United Kingdom General Strike and the Great Depression in the United Kingdom. Though fiction, it has many points in common with Raymond Williams's own background.

Matthew Price, a university lecturer in economic history, returns from London to visit his sick father in South Wales. The novel is set in the fictional village of Glynmawr in the Black Mountains, a rural area but closely connected to the nearby coal mining valleys of the South Wales coalfield. His father had been a railway signalman, and the story includes lengthy flashbacks to the 1920s and 1930s, including the General Strike and its impact on a small group of railway workers living in a community made up mostly of farmers.

It also describes Matthew Price's decision to leave his own community, studying at Cambridge before becoming a lecturer in London.

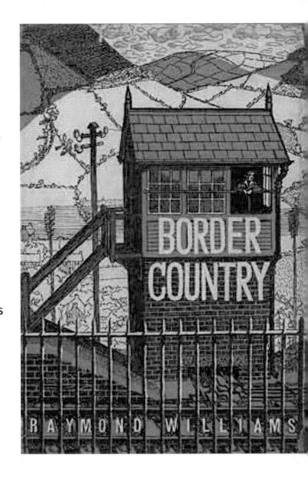

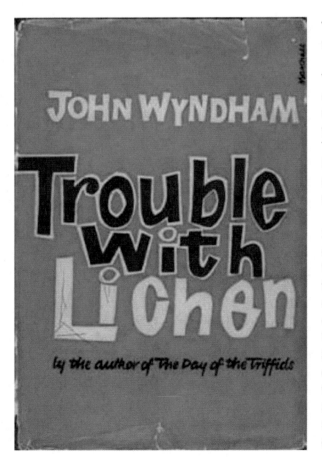

Trouble with Lichen (published 1960) is a science fiction novel by British writer John Wyndham.

The plot concerns a young female biochemist that discovers that a chemical extracted from an unusual strain of lichen can be used to slow down the ageing process, enabling people to live to around 200–300 years. Wyndham speculates how society would deal with this prospect. The two central characters are Diana Brackley and Francis Saxover, two biochemists who run parallel investigations into the properties of a specific species of lichen after Diana notices that a trace of the specimen prevents some milk turning sour.

She and Francis separately manage to extract from the lichen a new drug, dubbed Antigerone, which slows down the body's ageing process. While Francis uses it only on himself and his immediate family (without their knowledge), Diana founds a cosmetic spa, and builds up a clientele of some of the most powerful women in England, giving them low doses of Antigerone, preserving their beauty and youth.

When Francis finds out about the spas, he erroneously assumes that Diana's motive is profit. Diana's aim, however, is actually female empowerment, intending to gain the support of these influential women, believing that if Antigerone became publicly known, it would be reserved only for the men in power. After a customer suffers an allergic reaction to one of Diana's products, the secret of the drug begins to emerge.

The Sot-Weed Factor is a 1960 novel by the American writer John Barth. The novel marks the beginning of Barth's literary postmodernism. The Sot-Weed Factor takes its title from the poem The Sot-weed Factor, or A Voyage to Maryland, A Satyr (1708) by the English-born poet Ebenezer Cooke (c. 1665 – c. 1732), of whom few biographical details are known.

A satirical epic set in the 1680s–90s in London and colonial Maryland, the novel tells of a fictionalized Ebenezer Cooke, who is given the title "Poet Laureate of Maryland" by Charles Calvert, 3rd Baron Baltimore and commissioned to write a Marylandiad to sing the praises of the colony. He undergoes adventures on his journey to and within Maryland while striving to preserve his virginity. The complicated Tom Jones-like plot is interwoven with numerous digressions and stories-within-stories, and is written in a style patterned on the writing of 18th-century novelists such as Henry Fielding, Laurence Sterne and Tobias Smollett. The novel is a satirical epic of the colonization of Maryland based on the life of an actual poet, Ebenezer Cooke, who wrote a poem of the same title. The Sot-Weed Factor is what Northrop Frye called an anatomy—a large, loosely structured work, with digressions, distractions, stories within stories, and lists.

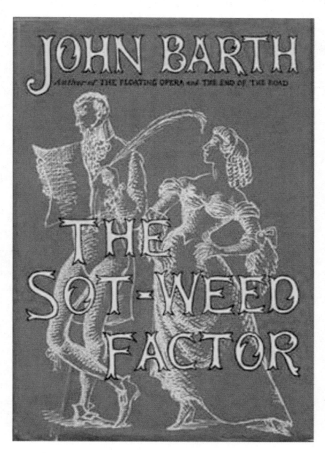

Rogue Moon is a short science fiction novel by American writer Algis Budrys, published in 1960. It was a 1961 Hugo Award nominee. A substantially cut version of the novel was originally published in F&SF; this novella-length story was included in The Science Fiction Hall of Fame, Volume Two, edited by Ben Bova. It was adapted into a radio drama by Yuri Rasovsky in 1979.

Rogue Moon is largely about the discovery and investigation of a large alien artifact found on the surface of the Moon. The object eventually kills its explorers in various ways—more specifically, investigators "die in their effort to penetrate an alien-built labyrinth where one wrong turn means instant death", but their deaths slowly reveal the funhouse-like course humans must take in moving through it.

In contemporary reviews, Alfred Bester called Rogue Moon "one of the finest flashes of heat lightning to dazzle us this year," saying it "has come very close to realizing our ideal of science fiction, the story of how human beings may be affected by the science of the future." Bester, however, faulted the ending as unresolved, declaring that Budrys "brought his book to a semi-cadence at exactly the point where it cried for completion.

To Kill a Mockingbird is a novel by Harper Lee published in 1960. Instantly successful, widely read in high schools and middle schools in the United States, it has become a classic of modern American literature, winning the Pulitzer Prize. The plot and characters are loosely based on Lee's observations of her family, her neighbors and an event that occurred near her hometown of Monroeville, Alabama, in 1936, when she was 10 years old.

The novel is renowned for its warmth and humor, despite dealing with the serious issues of rape and racial inequality. The narrator's father, Atticus Finch, has served as a moral hero for many readers and as a model of integrity for lawyers. Historian, J. Crespino explains, "In the twentieth century, To Kill a Mockingbird is probably the most widely read book dealing with race in America, and its main character, Atticus Finch, the most enduring fictional image of racial heroism."

To Kill a Mockingbird was Lee's only published book until Go Set a Watchman, an earlier draft of To Kill a Mockingbird, was published on July 14, 2015. Lee continued to respond to her work's impact until her death in February 2016, although she had refused any personal publicity for herself or the novel since 1964.

A Canticle for Leibowitz is a post-apocalyptic science fiction novel by American writer Walter M. Miller Jr., first published in 1959. Set in a Catholic monastery in the desert of the southwestern United States after a devastating nuclear war, the book spans thousands of years as civilization rebuilds itself. The monks of the Albertian Order of Leibowitz preserve the surviving remnants of man's scientific knowledge until the world is again ready for it.

The novel is a fixup of three short stories Miller published in The Magazine of Fantasy & Science Fiction that were inspired by the author's participation in the bombing of the monastery at the Battle of Monte Cassino during World War II.

The book is considered one of the classics of science fiction and has never been out of print. Appealing to mainstream and genre critics and readers alike, it won the 1961 Hugo Award for best science fiction novel, and its themes of religion, recurrence, and church versus state have generated a significant body of scholarly research. A sequel, Saint Leibowitz and the Wild Horse Woman, was published posthumously in 1997.

THE 1960 OSCARS

BEST ACTOR

Burt Lancaster   Elmer Gantry

BEST ACTRESS

Elizabeth Taylor   Butterfield 8

BEST DIRECTOR

Billy Wilder   The Apartment

BEST MOTION PICTURE

The Apartment   Billy Wilder

BEST SUPPORTING ACTOR

Peter Ustinov   Spartacus

BEST SUPPORTING ACTRESS

Shirley Jones   Elmer Gantry

BEST STORY AND SCREENPLAY

The Apartment   Billy Wilder

BEST MUSIC SCORE

Exodus   Ernest Gold

BEST SCORING OF A MUSICAL PICTURE BEST SONG

Song Without End   Morris Stoloff and Harry Sukman

BEST SONG

"Never on Sunday" from Never on Sunday   Manos Hatzidakis

BEST SOUND

The Alamo   Gordon E. Sawyer and Fred Hynes

BEST CINEMATOGRAPHY

Spartacus   Russell Metty

BEST SPECIAL EFFECTS

The Time Machine   Gene Warren and Tim Baar

The 33rd Academy Awards, honoring the best in film for 1960, were held on April 17, 1961, at the Santa Monica Civic Auditorium in Santa Monica, California. They were hosted by Bob Hope. This was the first ceremony to be aired on ABC television, which has aired the Academy Awards ever since (save for the period between 1971 and 1975, when they were aired on NBC for the first time since the previous year.)

The Apartment was the last black-and-white film to win Best Picture until Schindler's List (1993).

Young and rising star Hayley Mills was selected by the Academy Board of Governors to be the year's recipient of the Academy Juvenile Award for her breakthrough and acclaimed performance in Walt Disney's production of Pollyanna.

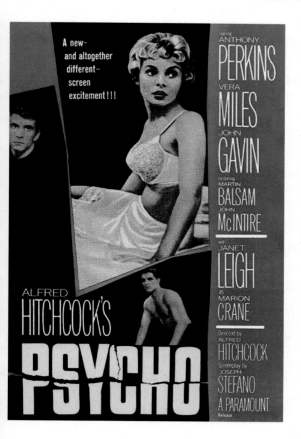

Psycho. Phoenix office worker Marion Crane is fed up with the way life has treated her. She has to meet her lover Sam in lunch breaks, and they cannot get married because Sam has to give most of his money away in alimony.

One Friday, Marion is trusted to bank forty thousand dollars by her employer. Seeing the opportunity to take the money and start a new life, Marion leaves town and heads towards Sam's California store. Tired after the long drive and caught in a storm, she gets off the main highway and pulls into the Bates Motel. The motel is managed by a quiet young man called Norman who seems to be dominated by his mother.

Box Office
Budget:$806,947 (estimated)
Gross USA: $32,000,000
Cumulative Worldwide Gross: $50,000,000, 31 January 2004

Run time is 1h 49mins.

Trivia

Director Sir Alfred Hitchcock was so pleased with the score written by Bernard Herrmann, that he doubled the composer's salary to $34,501. Hitchcock later said, "Thirty-three percent of the effect of Psycho was due to the music."

When the cast and crew began work on the first day, they had to raise their right hands and promise not to divulge one word of the story. Sir Alfred Hitchcock also withheld the ending part of the script from his cast until he needed to shoot it.

Director Sir Alfred Hitchcock originally envisioned the shower sequence as completely silent, but Bernard Herrmann went ahead and scored it anyway, and upon hearing it, Hitchcock immediately changed his mind.

Goofs

When Norman first meets Marion his first words to her were an apology for not hearing her on account of the rain. He then asks her to accompany him into the office. His lips don't even move during this scene and he gestures with a hand signal for her to go inside instead; the audio must have been added later in post-production.

The calendar belonging to the Chief of Police reads '17' on December 20th.

Janet Leigh's body double is obvious when Norman is pulling Marion from the tub onto the shower curtain; the dead woman has painted toenails while Janet had clear nails during the stabbing shots.

The Time Machine. On the 5th January 1900, a disheveled looking H.G. Wells - George to his friends - arrives late to his own dinner party. He tells his guests of his travels in his time machine, the work about which his friends knew. They were also unbelieving and skeptical of any practical use if it did indeed work. George knew that his machine was stationary in geographic position, but he did not account for changes in what happens over time to that location. He also learns that the machine is not impervious and he is not immune to those who do not understand him or the machine's purpose. George tells his friends that he did not find the Utopian society he so wished had developed. He mentions specifically a civilization several thousand years into the future which consists of the subterranean morlocks and the surface dwelling eloi, who on first glance lead a carefree life. Despite all these issues, love can still bloom over the spread of millennia.

Box Office
Budget:$750,000 (estimated)
Gross USA: $3,509,800, 31 December 1960
Cumulative Worldwide Gross: $5,689,800, 31 December 1960

Run time is 1h 43mins.

Trivia
Yvette Mimieux was actually underage when shooting began (she turned 18 during the shoot) and was not legally supposed to work a full shooting schedule, but did. She was inexperienced, but as she worked on this film she kept getting better and better, so that by the end of the shoot the producers went back and re-shot some of her earliest scenes.

When the Time Traveler stops in 1966, in the front window of Filby's Department store there is a very brief shot of a display featuring "the latest tubeless TV". It looks remarkably like a modern flat-panel computer monitor.

The "lava" in the volcano scene in downtown was actually oatmeal with orange and red food coloring spilled onto a platform and slowly moved down the miniature set.

The miniature version of the Time Machine was kept by producer-director George Pal. It was lost when Pal's home was destroyed by fire.

Goofs
In the opening shot of the street outside George's house, the post-box bears the initials G.R. British Royal Mail post-boxes bear the initials of the reigning monarch at the time they were installed. G.R. indicates King George V, who did not become monarch until 1910 - some 10 years after the scene is set.

When the atomic bomb explodes in 1966 London, all the buildings, cars, etc., are instantly incinerated; but in close-up George is shown lying flat on perfect, unburned green grass, unscathed, and the time machine is equally undamaged, sitting undisturbed beside blossoming, untouched foliage.

The Magnificent Seven. A remake of "The Seven Samurai." Seven men are picked to defend a Mexican village from banditos that come every now and then to take whatever the town has grown since their last visit.

When they are hired, they go to the town and teach the villagers how to defend themselves. When the leader of the bandits comes, they fight him and his men off. The second time he comes, the villagers give the seven to them, due to a heated argument.

The leader of the bandits takes their guns and throws them out of town. He gives them horses and gives their guns back to them when they are far out of town. The seven decide that they aren't going to run, and head back to the village for a final showdown.

Box Office
Budget:$2,000,000 (estimated)
Gross USA: $4,905,000

Run time 2h 8mins.

Trivia
Yul Brynner had a major say in casting decisions, including the decision to cast Steve McQueen. He specifically requested that McQueen be cast as Vin Tanner. Brynner later regretted the move since he and McQueen developed a disastrous relationship on set.

In later years, Yul Brynner and Steve McQueen reconciled. McQueen, dying of cancer, called Brynner to thank him. "What for?" queried Brynner. "You coulda had me kicked off the movie when I rattled you," replied McQueen, "but you let me stay and that picture made me, so thanks". Brynner told him, "I am the king and you are the rebel prince: every bit as royal . . . and dangerous to cross." McQueen said, "I had to make it up with Yul cause without him I wouldn't have been in that picture."

Yul Brynner (5'10") was concerned to make sure he always appeared substantially taller than Steve McQueen (5'9-1/2"), to the point of making a little mound of earth and standing on it in all their shots together. McQueen, for his part, casually kicked at the mound every time he passed by it.

Goofs
The knife used by Britt appears to be a stiletto switchblade (automatic opening knife with locking mechanism). This kind of weapon was brought from Italy only in the '50s which is about 100 years later than the action of this movie.

Steve McQueen wears Levi jeans with the famous red tab. These were introduced in the 1930's. Decades after the setting of this movie.

Steve McQueen is wearing a wedding ring throughout the movie.

Spartacus. In 73 B.C., a Thracian slave leads a revolt at a gladiatorial school run by Lentulus Batiatus (Sir Peter Ustinov). The uprising soon spreads across the Italian Peninsula involving thousands of slaves. The plan is to acquire sufficient funds to acquire ships from Silesian pirates who could then transport them to other lands from Brandisium in the south. The Roman Senator Gracchus (Charles Laughton) schemes to have Marcus Publius Glabrus (John Dall), Commander of the garrison of Rome, lead an army against the slaves who are living on Vesuvius. When Glabrus is defeated his mentor, Senator and General Marcus Licinius Crassus (Sir Laurence Olivier) is greatly embarrassed and leads his own army against the slaves. Spartacus and the thousands of freed slaves successfully make their way to Brandisium only to find that the Silesians have abandoned them. They then turn north and must face the might of Rome.

Box Office
Budget:$12,000,000 (estimated)
Gross USA: $30,000,000
Cumulative Worldwide Gross: $60,000,000, 1 January 1998

Run time 2h 24mins.

Trivia
Stanley Kubrick was brought in as director after Kirk Douglas had a major falling out with the original director, Anthony Mann. According to Sir Peter Ustinov, the salt mines sequence was the only footage shot by Mann.

Stanley Kubrick spent forty thousand dollars on the over-ten-acre gladiator camp set. On the side of the set that bordered the freeway, a one hundred twenty-five-foot asbestos curtain was erected in order to film the burning of the camp, which was organized with collaboration from the Los Angeles Fire and Police Departments. Studio press materials state that five thousand uniforms, and seven tons of armor were borrowed from Italian museums, and that every one of Hollywood's one hundred eighty-seven stuntmen was trained in the gladiatorial rituals of combat to the death. Modern sources note that the production utilized approximately ten thousand five hundred people.

Stanley Kubrick wanted Audrey Hepburn to play Varinia.

Goofs
A truck drives along the hills behind a battle scene.

Many of the horsemen use stirrups, an invention which did not reach Europe until about the 7th century A.D., and eight centuries after the film is set.

Slaves digging with steel shovels of a pattern invented in the early 20th century instead of Roman wooden spades.

Antoninus is wearing a Rolex watch.

Movie-wise,
there
has
never
been
anything
like "THE APARTMENT"
love-wise,
laugh-wise
or
otherwise-wise!
Jack
Lemmon
Shirley
MacLaine
Fred
MacMurray
Ray Walston Edie Adams

The Apartment. As of the 1st November 1959, mild mannered C.C. Baxter has been working at Consolidated Life, an insurance company, for close to four years, and is one of close to thirty-two thousand employees located in their Manhattan head office. To distinguish himself from all the other lowly cogs in the company in the hopes of moving up the corporate ladder, he often works late, but only because he can't get into his apartment, located off of Central Park West, since he has provided it to a handful of company executives - Messrs. Dobisch, Kirkeby, Vanderhoff and Eichelberger - on a rotating basis for their extramarital liaisons in return for a good word to the personnel director, Jeff D. Sheldrake. When Baxter is called into Sheldrake's office for the first time, he learns that it isn't just to be promoted as he expects, but also to add married Sheldrake to the list to who he will lend his apartment. What Baxter is unaware of is that Sheldrake's mistress is Fran Kubelik.

Box Office
Budget:$3,000,000 (estimated)
Gross USA: $18,600,000

Run time 1h 41mins.

Trivia

Billy Wilder originally thought of the idea for the film after seeing Brief Encounter (1945) and wondering about the plight of a character unseen in that film. Shirley MacLaine was only given forty pages of the script because Wilder didn't want her to know how the story would turn out. She thought it was because the script wasn't finished.

This was the last B&W movie to win Best Picture at The Academy Awards until The Artist (2011). Schindler's List (1993) which won in 1994 was not completely B&W as some scenes were in color, like the girl in the red and the candle at the beginning.

For this film, Billy Wilder became the first person to win the Academy Awards for Best Picture, Best Director and Best Screenplay.

Goofs

When Kirkeby returns to the apartment to look for the galoshes left behind by Sylvia, he first looks carefully behind the chair to the right of the fireplace, then he goes to the left of the fireplace to look behind another chair, then he returns to the right of the fireplace to pick up the galoshes behind the chair where he already looked when he first came in.

The frozen daiquiri in the cocktail lounge melts, reforms, and melts again.

At the very end of the film, Baxter and Fran sit down to play a game of Gin. This game is played with 10 cards dealt to each player, but Baxter deals at least 13 cards to both Fran and himself before the picture finally fades out.

La Dolce Vita. Basking in the allure of early-1960s Rome and bustling Via Veneto's elegant sybarites and cosmopolitan celebrities, the hopeful writer and now a stylish columnist, Marcello Rubini, spends his nights looking for the next big story, or better still, a new excitement.

Balancing between hedonism and cynicism; self-loathing, and an irrepressible yearning for freedom and beauty, the philandering reporter will put his undeniable charm to the test, when the international film star and unattainable object of desire, Sylvia, arrives in town.
Now, against the backdrop of the eternal Fontana di Trevi, dreams burn down, as an undying hope for a better future gives way to a new set of enticements--this almost feral passion for life and an equally unquenched desire for love have always defined Marcello's thirsty existence. However, what is the price to pay for a hearty slice of the sweet life?

Box Office
Gross USA: $19,516,000

Run Time 2h 56mins.

Trivia

The famous scene in the Trevi Fountain was shot over a week in March, when nights were still cold. According to Federico Fellini (in an interview with Costanzo Costantini), Anita Ekberg stood in the cold water in her dress for hours without any trouble. Marcello Mastroianni, on the other hand, had to wear a wetsuit beneath his clothes, and even that wasn't enough. Still freezing, he downed an entire bottle of vodka, so that he was completely drunk while shooting the scene.

Credit for the creation of Steiner goes to co-screenwriter Tullio Pinelli. Having gone to school with Italian novelist Cesare Pavese, Pinelli had closely followed the writer's career and felt that his over-intellectualism had become emotionally sterile, leading to his suicide in a Turin hotel in 1950. This idea of a "burnt-out existence" is carried over to Steiner in the party episode where the sounds of nature are not to be experienced first-hand by himself and his guests but in the virtual world of tape recordings.

Goofs

When Marcello is typewriting in a restaurant on the beach and talking to the blonde young girl, the bar of the typewriter is centered on the machine. In the next take, it is displaced to the left of the typewriter.

The aircraft which brings Sylvia to Rome is an Alitalia Vickers Viscount as it comes in to land, but is both a Douglas DC-7C and DC-6B when it is on the ground.

At the top of St. Peter's dome the wind blows Sylvia's hat off. The wire on her hat used to achieve this effect is clearly visible trailing off to the right during the scene.

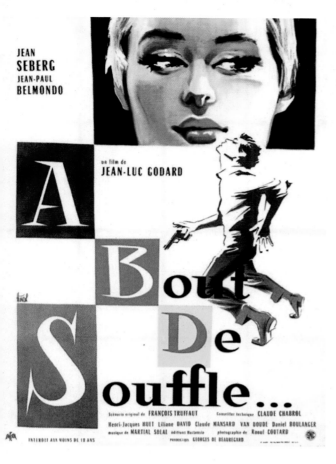

Breathless. Michel Poiccard, an irresponsible sociopath and small-time thief, steals a car and impulsively murders the motorcycle policeman who pursues him. Now wanted by the authorities, he renews his relationship with Patricia Franchini, a hip American girl studying journalism at the Sorbonne, whom he had met in Nice a few weeks earlier.

Before leaving Paris, he plans to collect a debt from an underworld acquaintance and expects her to accompany him on his planned getaway to Italy. Even with his face in the local papers and media, Poiccard seems oblivious to the dragnet that is slowly closing around him as he recklessly pursues his love of American movies and libidinous interest in the beautiful American.

Box Office
Budget: FRF 400,000 (estimated) French Francs
Opening Weekend USA: $3,222,
23 April 2000, Limited Release
Gross USA: $336,705, 31 October 2010

Run time 1h 30mins.

Trivia
According to Jean-Pierre Melville, Godard asked him for consultation during the post-production stage because the first edit was too long for distribution. Melville suggested Godard remove all scenes that slowed down the action (his own turn as novelist Parvulesco included). But instead of excluding entire scenes, Godard cut little bits from here and there. This led to the "jump cut" technique this movie introduced. Melville declared the result to be excellent.

According to Raoul Coutard, some sleight of hand was involved in getting a permit to shoot on the streets of Paris. A complete script was needed to obtain the permit, so Jean-Luc Godard had an assistant type up a mock script for a film that would never be shot.

To give a more detached, spontaneous quality, Jean-Luc Godard fed the actors their lines as scenes were being filmed.

Jean-Luc Godard would write the script in the morning of each day of filming without the assistance of the script supervisor. He would write his notes into an exercise book which he would allow only the actors to see

Goofs
When Patricia (Jean Seberg) is going up the escalator, a plant beside it can be seen moving as if knocked by the cameraman going up in front of her.

During street shots, countless passers-by keep on staring into the camera, revealing the shots to be made without appropriate filming barriers and not using extras for pedestrians.

"Easily the best British movie since 'Room At The Top'!"
TIME MAGAZINE

Bryanston presents A Woodfall Production starring **ALBERT FINNEY**
a film SHIRLEY ANNE FIELD · RACHEL ROBERTS and introducing HYLDA BAKER
From the novel by Alan Sillitoe · Produced by Harry Saltzman & Tony Richardson · Directed by Karel Reisz · Screenplay by Alan Sillitoe

Saturday Night and Sunday Morning. Arthur, one of Britain's angry young men of the 1960s, is a hardworking factory worker who slaves all week at his mindless job for his modest wages. Come Saturday night, he's off to the pub for a loud and rowdy beer session. With him is Brenda, his girlfriend of the moment.

Married to a fellow worker, she is nonetheless captivated by his rugged good looks and his devil-may-care attitude. Soon a new love interest Doreen enters and a week later, Brenda announces she's pregnant. She tells Arthur she needs money for an abortion, and Arthur promises to pay for it.

By this time, his relationship with Doreen has ripened and Brenda, hearing of it, confronts him. He denies everything, but it's obvious that their affair is all but over.

Box Office
Budget:£100,000 (estimated)

Run time 1h 29mins.

Trivia

British rock band the Arctic Monkeys were heavily influenced by this film. The title of their debut album "Whatever People Say I Am, That's What I'm Not" is a direct quote from the movie, and many of the songs were inspired by Albert Finney's character. Also the art design of the album was influenced by the realist images of British working class neighbourhoods and night life in "Saturday Night and Sunday Morning".

The censors were not too keen on the scene where Arthur wakes up on Sunday morning in bed with his mistress as the scene directly implies extra-marital sex, a notable first for British cinema.

The house used as the filming location for the Seaford's' house was owned by Alan Sillitoe, the author of the novel on which the film is based.

The factory scenes were filmed in the same factory that original author Alan Sillitoe worked in during the war when he was making shells and other artillery. At the time of filming, the factory was owned by the Raleigh bicycle company.

At the end of the film, Arthur and Doreen are sitting on a grassy bank overlooking a building site where an estate of new houses is being built. This was a film set built especially for the film in Wembley, London, by Nottingham builders Simms Sons & Cooke.

The name Skeggy is mentioned, this is a shortened name of the sea-side resort in Lincolnshire, of Skegness, which is a distance of some 78 miles from Nottingham.

Jack's motorcycle (with the sidecar) is a Norton ES2 c.1947-52.

Village of the Damned. In London, the military Alan Bernard is talking to his brother-in-law Gordon Zellaby in Midwich by telephone when there is a communication breakdown with the village. Alan heads to the British village and finds that all the inhabitants have fallen unconscious at the same time and who else crosses the borderline faints. Out of the blue, the inhabitants awake at the same time. Two months later Anthea Zellaby tells her husband Gordon that she is pregnant. But soon, the local Dr. Willers and Gordon realize that every woman in the village of childbearing age is pregnant. Anthea and the other women deliver perfect children and soon Dr. Willers note that all the children have strange eyes, short fingernails and different blond hair. Gordon also finds that his son David is a leader of the children that have no feelings and what one learns, the others also learn. Further they are capable to read and control minds and are a menace to the inhabitants of Midwich. Will Gordon be capable to keep the children under control?

Box Office
Budget:$200,000 (estimated)
Cumulative Worldwide Gross: $2,175,000, 31 December 1960

Run time 1h 55mins.

Trivia

The eerie effect of the children's glowing eyes was created by matting a negative (reversed) image of their eyes over the pupils when they used their powers. The British print of the film contained no optical effects as the British Board of Film Classification considered them too frightening for an 'A' classification.

Originally begun in 1957 as an American picture to star Ronald Colman, M-G-M had this scheduled for Spring 1958 and Spring 1959 and postponed both times. Coleman was gravely ill and housebound, dying soon after the script was completed, in an odd twist, his replacement was George Sanders, who had recently married Benita Hume, Colman's widow.

When the military are testing Midwich for radiation after everyone wakes up, there is a sign in the background that says "Beware of Children".

Goofs

Alan Bernard drives to Midwich on a clear, sunny day when he stops to talk to a policeman. But in the next shot of the road, it's overcast and misty.

The action takes place in the 1950s (some characters are wearing medal ribbons for the Korean War), but all of Major General Leighton's campaign ribbons predate 1939; he has no ribbons for World War Two. He could have retired before 1939, but he would have been far too old to rejoin after the war.

An abdominal X-ray is displayed which supposedly shows the fetus of a pregnant woman. Not only is there no fetus, the X-ray isn't even that of a woman, as the pelvis is obviously that of a man.

Swiss Family Robinson. A family in route to New Guinea is shipwrecked on a deserted tropical island. They are forced to remain on the island because of the damage to the ship and the pirates that are roaming the islands.

They create a home on the island (centering on a huge tree house) and explore the island and its wildlife. Plenty of adventure ensues as the family deals with issues of survival and pirates, and the brothers must learn how to live on the island with an uncertain future.

Director: Ken Annakin
Writers: Lowell S. Hawley (screenplay), Johann David Wyss (novel) (as Johann Wyss)
Stars: John Mills, Dorothy McGuire, James MacArthur

Box Office
Budget:$5,000,000 (estimated)
Gross USA: $40,356,000

Run time 1h 13mins.

Trivia

As revealed by Director Ken Annakin on the DVD commentary, the trapped zebra was subjected to electric shocks to make it move about, a practice that is now illegal in Hollywood movies.

Walt Disney Pictures bought the rights to the 1940 version produced and distributed by RKO, and then Walt Disney confiscated all known prints of RKO Radio Pictures' version, so there wouldn't be comparisons to the Disney version.

Walt Disney Pictures' first movie in Panavision.

Although set in a tropical paradise, the filming in Tobago was considerably hampered by almost constant rain.

Goofs

The crew is said to have abandoned the ship during the storm. This seems highly illogical. In the days before inflatable life rafts, the only escape vessels on board would have been small wooden life boats, similar to a canoe. It's hard to imagine a canoe fairing any better in a storm at sea than a large sailing vessel.

When we first get a shot of the Pirate King, he is wearing a Red Coat. Then, in the next shot, he's wearing a blue officer's coat. Colors are alternated throughout the movie.

When Fritz swings across the pool swapping vines halfway, just as he is landing on the rock, a crew member's hand reaches up into shot, just below his feet.

Oceans 11. Danny Ocean and his friend Jimmy Foster recruit their buddies to rob four of the biggest casinos in Las Vegas on New Year's Eve. The men are all known to one another and served in the Airborne during the war.

The plan is to knock out the electricity supply to the city and for their electrical expert, Tony Bergdorf, to set the wiring so that the activation of the emergency generators would open the doors to all of the cashier's offices.

The men take up jobs in the casinos - entertainers, waiters, busboys - and all goes well until Bergdorf has a heart attack just after the robbery. Not only does his death suggest to Jimmy Foster's soon to be father-in-law Duke Santos just who the robbers are, Danny and the men make an important mistake when they think they've found the perfect way to ship the money out of Las Vegas without getting caught.

Box Office
Budget:$2,800,000 (estimated)
Gross USA: $12,317,000

Run Time 2h 7mins.

Trivia

According to Frank Sinatra Jr. on the DVD Commentary, Sammy Davis Jr. was forced to stay at a "colored only" hotel during the filming because Las Vegas would not allow blacks to stay at the major hotels despite his appearing with Frank Sinatra, Dean Martin, and the others at the Sands Hotel. He was only allowed to stay at the major hotels after Frank Sinatra confronted the casino owners on his behalf, therefore breaking Vegas' unofficial color barrier.

In a scene between Danny (Frank Sinatra) and Adele (Patrice Wymore), Adele throws a dish of candy at Danny. The throwing of the dish was ad-libbed, which accounts for the genuine look of surprise on Sinatra's face and the faces of his co-stars.

Steve McQueen turned down a role on the advice of his friend Hedda Hopper, who told him to be his own man rather than Frank Sinatra's "flunky".

Goofs

When Sam Harmon is singing 'Ain't That a Kick in the Head', a trumpet solo is featured most prominently, but the jazz combo on stage has no trumpet player. Instead, there is a saxophonist who mimes his part.

In the scene where Danny gives his mistress his room key, in the background a so-called professional roulette dealer tries to spin the ball and fails. He snatches the ball out again and fails again. In a third attempt, he somehow makes the ball go around the rim as it should. The actor playing the dealer has obviously never thrown a roulette ball in his life.

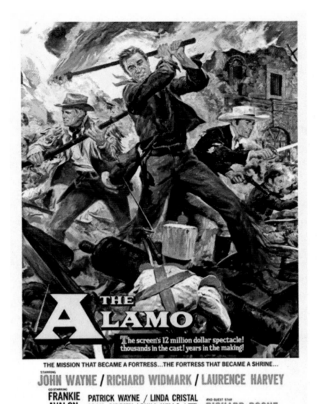

The Alamo. In 1836, General Santa Anna and the Mexican Army are sweeping across Texas. To be able to stop him, General Sam Houston needs time to get his main force into shape. To buy that time he orders Colonel William Travis to defend a small mission on the Mexicans' route at all costs. Travis' small troop is swelled by groups accompanying Jim Bowie and Davy Crockett, but as the situation becomes ever more desperate Travis makes it clear there will be no shame if they leave while they can.

An Oscar winner for Best Sound.
Golden Globe winner for Best Original Score

Box Office
Budget:$12,000,000 (estimated)
Gross USA: $17,262,932

Director: John Wayne
Writer: James Edward Grant (original screenplay)
Stars: John Wayne, Richard Widmark, Laurence Harvey

Run Time 2h 42mins.

Trivia
John Wayne originally intended that Richard Widmark should play Davy Crockett, while Wayne himself would have taken the small role of Sam Houston so he could focus his energy on directing the picture. However, Wayne was only able to get financial backing if he played one of the main parts, so he decided to play Crockett and cast Widmark as Jim Bowie.

John Wayne partially financed this film himself. During shooting, the film was delayed due to various production problems. Wayne was under so much pressure, he smoked cigarettes almost non-stop when not acting.

Charlton Heston was among the actors who were sent the script and John Wayne wanted him to play Jim Bowie. Heston later said there seemed good reasons for him not to do the film and, when pressed further, stated having John Wayne as director to be one of them. Heston had just spent months filming Ben-Hur (1959) and did not want to commit to another large epic.

Goofs
The movie makes an attempt to recreate the iconic bell-shaped facade of the church, but in fact, that was not added until 1850 by the U.S. Army. At the time of the battle, the roof of the church was flat all the way around the entire structure.

Susannah Dickinson's dresses have an obvious zipper. Zippers weren't invented until 1914 and weren't used on dresses until the 1930s.

During the final attack one of Santa Anna's men appears to throw a hand grenade into a fort building which immediately explodes.

MUSIC 1960

The Billboard Hot 100 chart is the main song chart of the American music industry and is updated every week by the Billboard magazine. During 1958–1970 the chart was based collectively on each single's weekly physical sales figures and airplay on American radio stations.

January 4, 1960	Marty Robbins	"El Paso"	2
January 18, 1960	Johnny Preston	"Running Bear"	3
February 8, 1960	Mark Dinning	"Teen Angel"	1
February 22, 1960	Percy Faith	"Theme from 'A Summer Place'"	9
April 25, 1960	Elvis Presley	"Stuck on You"	4
May 23, 1960	The Everly Brothers	"Cathy's Clown"	5
June 27, 1960	Connie Francis	"Everybody's Somebody's Fool"	2
July 11, 1960	Hollywood Argyles	"Alley-Oop"	1
July 18, 1960	Brenda Lee	"I'm Sorry"	3
August 8, 1960	Brian Hyland	"Itsy Bitsy Teenie Weenie Yellow Polka Dot Bikini"	1
August 15, 1960	Elvis Presley	"It's Now or Never"	5
September 19, 1960	Chubby Checker	"The Twist"	1
September 26, 1960	Connie Francis	"My Heart Has a Mind of Its Own"	2
October 10, 1960	Larry Verne	"Mr. Custer"	1
October 17, 1960	The Drifters	"Save the Last Dance for Me"	3
October 24, 1960	Brenda Lee	"I Want to Be Wanted"	1
November 14, 1960	Ray Charles	"Georgia on My Mind"	1
November 21, 1960	Maurice Williams and the Zodiacs	"Stay"	1
November 28, 1960	Elvis Presley	"Are You Lonesome Tonight?"	6

Marty Robbins

"El Paso

"El Paso" is a country and western ballad written and originally recorded by Marty Robbins, and first released on Gunfighter Ballads and Trail Songs in September 1959. It was released as a single the following month, and became a major hit on both the country and pop music charts, reaching No. 1 in both at the start of 1960. It won the Grammy Award for Best Country & Western Recording in 1961, and remains Robbins' best-known song. It is widely considered a genre classic for its gripping narrative which ends in the death of its protagonist, its shift from past to present tense, haunting harmonies by vocalists Bobby Sykes and Jim Glaser (of the Glaser Brothers) and the eloquent and varied Spanish guitar accompaniment by Grady Martin that lends the recording a distinctive Tex-Mex feel.

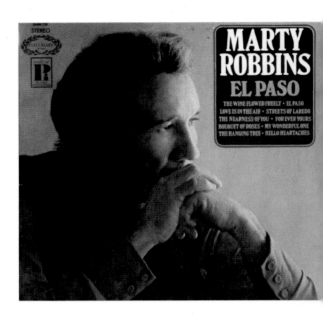

Johnny Preston

"Running Bear"

"Running Bear" is a song written by Jiles Perry Richardson (a.k.a. The Big Bopper) and sung most famously by Johnny Preston in 1959. The 1959 recording featured background vocals by Richardson, George Jones, and the session's producer Bill Hall, who provided the "Indian chanting" of "uga-uga" during the three verses, as well as the "Indian war cries" at the start and end of the record. It was No. 1 for three weeks in January 1960 on the Billboard Hot 100 in the United States. The song also reached No. 1 in the UK Singles Chart in 1960. Coincidentally, "Running Bear" was immediately preceded in the Hot 100 No. 1 position by Marty Robbins' "El Paso". Johnny Preston was signed to Mercury Records, and "Running Bear" was released in August 1959, seven months after Richardson's death in the plane crash that also killed Buddy Holly and Ritchie Valens.

Mark Dinning

"Teen Angel"

"Teen Angel" is a teenage tragedy song written by Jean Dinning (1924–2011) and her husband, Red Surrey, and performed by Jean's brother, Mark Dinning, and Alex Murray in 1959. "Teen Angel" was released in October 1959. The song was not an instant success, with radio stations in the U.S. banning the song, considering it too sad.

Despite the reluctance of radio stations, the song continued to climb the charts. In the last week of 1959, the single jumped from #100 to #50 on the Billboard Hot 100 chart. It went on to reach #1 on the U.S. Billboard Hot 100 (February 1960) and number thirty-seven in the UK Singles Chart (even though it was banned from being played by the BBC). Billboard ranked it as the No. 5 song of 1960.

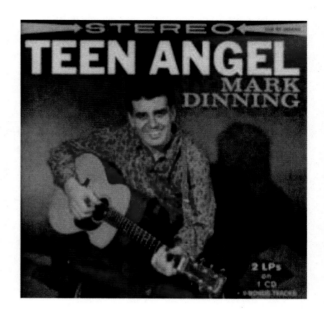

Percy Faith

" Theme from A Summer Place"

"Theme from A Summer Place" is a song with lyrics by Mack Discant and music by Max Steiner, written for the 1959 film A Summer Place, which starred Sandra Dee and Troy Donahue. It was recorded for the film as an instrumental by Hugo Winterhalter. Originally known as the "Molly and Johnny Theme", the piece is not the main title theme of the film, but a secondary love theme for the characters played by Dee and Donahue. Following its initial film appearance, the theme has been recorded by many artists in both instrumental and vocal versions, and has also appeared in a number of subsequent films and television programs. The best-known cover version of the theme is an instrumental version by Percy Faith and his orchestra that was a Number One hit for nine weeks on the Billboard Hot 100 chart in 1960.

Elvis Presley

"Stuck on You"

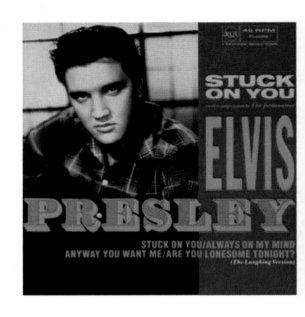

"Stuck on You" was Elvis Presley's first hit single after his two-year stint in the US Army, reaching number one in 1960 in the US. He recorded the song during March 1960, and the single was released within weeks and went to number one on the Billboard Hot 100 chart in late-April 1960, becoming his first number-one single of the 1960s and thirteenth overall. "Stuck on You" peaked at number six on the R&B chart. The song knocked Percy Faith's "Theme from A Summer Place" from the top spot, ending its nine-week run at number one on the chart. The record reached number three in the UK. The single had a special picture sleeve with the RCA Victor logo and catalog number on the top right corner and included, in large letters, "ELVIS" in red on the top right.

The Everly Brothers

"Cathy's Clown"

"Cathy's Clown" was The Everly Brothers' first single for Warner Bros., after they had recorded for Archie Bleyer's Cadence label for three years. It sold eight million copies worldwide, spending five weeks at number 1 on the U.S. Billboard Hot 100 chart and one week on the R&B chart.

The song spent seven weeks at number 1 on the UK Singles Chart in May and June 1960, and was the Everly Brothers' biggest-selling single and their third and final U.S. number 1 hit. Billboard ranked it as the number 3 song of the year for 1960.

In 2004, it was ranked 149th on Rolling Stone magazine's list of the 500 Greatest Songs of All Time.

Connie Francis

"Everybody's Somebody's Fool"

"Everybody's Somebody's Fool" is a song written by Jack Keller and Howard Greenfield that was a No. 1 hit for Connie Francis in 1960. A polka-style version in German, "Die Liebe ist ein seltsames Spiel", was the first German single recorded and released by Connie Francis, and it reached No. 1 on the single chart in 1960 in West Germany. "Everybody's Somebody's Fool" was written as a bluesy ballad, and the song was recorded at Olmstead Studios (NYC) during the 1960 recording session when Francis cut the song with the Joe Sherman Orchestra. The arrangement performed by Connie Francis is noted for its organ introduction. The song originally recorded by Connie Francis entitled "Everybody's Somebody's Fool" is often confused with an earlier song of the same title written by Ace Adams and Regina Adams.

Hollywood Argyles

"Alley Oop"

"Alley-Oop" is a song written and composed by Dallas Frazier in 1957. The song was inspired by the V. T. Hamlin-created comic strip of the same name.

The Hollywood Argyles, a short-lived studio band, recorded the song in 1960, and it reached #1 on the Billboard Hot 100 and #3 on the US R&B chart. It also went to #24 on the UK chart. It was produced by Gary Paxton, who also sang lead vocals. At the time, Paxton was under contract to Brent Records, where he recorded as Flip of Skip & Flip. Also in 1960, Dante & the Evergreens released a version that went to #15 on the Billboard Hot 100, while The Dyna-Sores released a version that went to #59 on the same chart. Both Dante & The Evergreens' and The Hollywood Argyles' versions were credited as number ones in Cash Box magazine's singles chart.

Brenda Lee

"I'm Sorry"

"I'm Sorry" is a 1960 hit song by 15-year-old American singer Brenda Lee. It peaked at No. 1 on the Billboard Hot 100 singles chart in July 1960. AllMusic guide wrote that it is the pop star's "definitive song", and one of the "finest teen pop songs of its era". It was written by Dub Allbritten and Ronnie Self. On the UK Singles Chart, the song peaked at No.12. According to the Billboard Book of Number One Hits by Fred Bronson, Brenda Lee recorded the song early in 1960, but her label, Decca Records, held it from release for several months out of concern that a 15-year-old girl was not mature enough to sing about unrequited love. When the song finally was released, it was considered to be the flip side of the more up-tempo "That's All You Gotta Do". Although "That's All You Gotta Do" was a chart success in its own right, reaching No. 6 on the Hot 100, it was "I'm Sorry" that became the smash hit and the standard.

Brian Hyland

"Itsy Bitsy Teenie Weenie Yellow Polkadot Bikini"

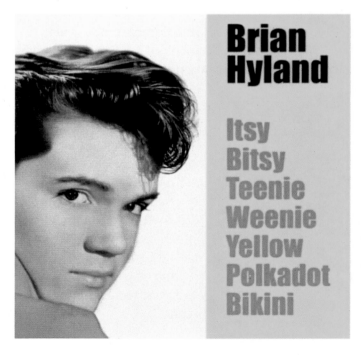

"Itsy Bitsy Teenie Weenie Yellow Polkadot Bikini" is a novelty song telling the story of a shy girl wearing a revealing polka dot bikini at the beach. It was written by Paul Vance and Lee Pockriss and first released in June 1960 by Brian Hyland, with orchestra conducted by John Dixon. The Hyland version reached number one on the Billboard Hot 100, selling a million copies in the US, and was a worldwide hit. The song has been adapted into French as "Itsy bitsy petit bikini" and into German as "Itsy Bitsy Teenie Weenie Honolulu-Strand-Bikini", reaching number one on national charts in both languages. Several versions of the song have proved successful in various European countries. In 1990 a version by British pop band Bombalurina, titled "Itsy Bitsy Teeny Weeny Yellow Polka Dot Bikini", reached number one on the UK Singles Chart and in Ireland.

Elvis Presley

"It's Now or Never"

"It's Now or Never" is a song recorded by Elvis Presley and released as a single in 1960. The song is the best-selling single by Presley (20 million copies), and one of the best-selling singles of all time. It was recorded by Bill Porter at RCA Studio B in Nashville. It is written in E major and has a tempo of 80 BPM.

In 1960, "It's Now or Never" was a number-one record in the U.S. for Elvis Presley, spending five weeks at number one and the UK, where it spent eight weeks at the top in 1960 and an additional week at number one in 2005 as a re-issue, and numerous other countries, selling in excess of 25 million copies worldwide, Elvis Presley's biggest international single ever. Its British release was delayed for some time because of rights issues, allowing the song to build up massive advance orders and to enter the UK Singles Chart at number one.

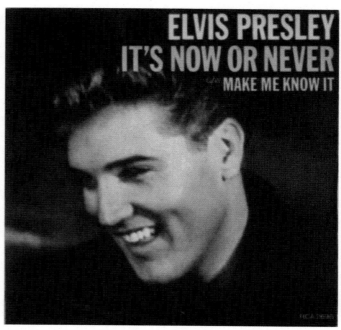

Chubby Checker

"The Twist"

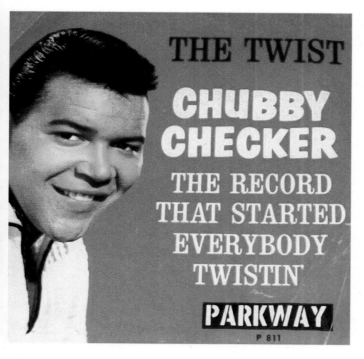

"The Twist" is an American pop song written and originally released in early 1959 (having been recorded on November 11, 1958) by Hank Ballard and the Midnighters as a B-side to "Teardrops on Your Letter". Ballard's version was a moderate 1960 hit, peaking at number 28 on the Billboard Hot 100. Chubby Checker's 1960 cover version of the song gave birth to the Twist dance craze. His single became a hit, reaching number 1 on the Billboard Hot 100 on September 19, 1960, where it stayed for one week, and setting a record as the only song to reach number 1 in two different hit parade runs when it resurfaced and topped the popular hit parade again for two weeks starting on January 13, 1962In 1988, "The Twist" again became popular due to a new recording of the song by The Fat Boys featuring Chubby Checker. This version reached number 2 in the United Kingdom and number 1 in Germany.

Connie Francis

"My Heart Has a Mind of Its Own" is

"My Heart Has a Mind of Its Own" is a song written by Howard Greenfield and Jack Keller which was a #1 hit for Connie Francis in 1960. Francis recorded "My Heart Has a Mind of Its Own" at Radio Recorders studio in Hollywood over three different sessions on July 9, 25, and 31, 1960 with Jesse Kaye and Arnold Maxin acting as producers; Gus Levene arranged the orchestration and conducted. Jack Keller brought one of the LA tapes back to New York for a Sax & Guitar overdub at Olmstead Studios. Artie Kaplan and Al Gorgoni were brought in for the sax and guitar overdub. "My Heart Has a Mind of Its Own" became Francis' second consecutive A-side to top the Billboard Hot 100 reaching #1 on the chart dated 26 September 1960 and holding there the following week. The single also marked Francis' final appearance of the R&B charts at #11.

Elvis Presley

"It's Now Or Never"

"Mr. Custer" is a march novelty song, sung by Larry Verne, and written by Al De Lory, Fred Darian, and Joseph Van Winkle. It was a No. 1 song in the United States in 1960, topping the Billboard Hot 100 singles chart for the issue dated October 10, 1960, and remained there for one week. It also reached No. 1 in Canada, September 12, 1960. It is a comical song about a soldier's plea to General Custer before the climactic Battle of the Little Bighorn against the Sioux, which he did not want to fight.[1] In 1964, Verne recorded and released a sequel novelty song entitled "Return of Mr. Custer," which used the same melody and music arrangement but failed to chart.

"Mr. Custer" was also a No. 12 success in the UK Singles Chart for Charlie Drake in 1960, his third such chart hit.

The Drifters

"Save The Last Dance For Me"

"Save the Last Dance for Me" is a song written by Doc Pomus and Mort Shuman, first recorded in 1960 by the Drifters, with Ben E. King on lead vocals.

In a 1990 interview, songwriter Doc Pomus tells the story of the song being recorded by the Drifters and originally designated as the B-side of the record. He credits Dick Clark with turning the record over and realizing "Save The Last Dance" was the stronger song.

The Drifters' version of the song, released a few months after Ben E. King left the group, would go on to spend three non-consecutive weeks at #1 on the U.S. pop chart, in addition to logging one week atop the U.S. R&B chart. In the UK The Drifters' recording reached #2 in December 1960.

Connie Francis

"My Heart Has a Mind of Its Own" is

'I Want to Be Wanted" is a popular song sung by Brenda Lee that was a number-one song in the United States during the year 1960. It topped the Billboard Hot 100 singles chart for the issue dated October 24, 1960, and remained there for one week. It is an Italian song, Per tutta a vita (For all lifetime), that was in the original version of Never on Sunday.

This was Brenda Lee's second number-one single, her first being "I'm Sorry". The English lyrics of "I Want to Be Wanted" were written by Kim Gannon.

Andy Williams released a version as the B-side to his single "Stranger on the Shore". The song was covered by Olivia Newton-John on her 1992 album Back to Basics: The Essential Collection 1971–1992.

Ray Charles

"Georgia On My Mind"

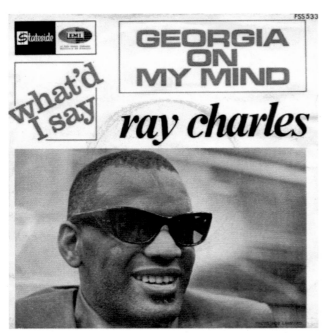

"Georgia on My Mind" is a 1930 song written by Hoagy Carmichael and Stuart Gorrell and first recorded that year. It has often been associated with Ray Charles, a native of the U.S. state of Georgia, who recorded it for his 1960 album The Genius Hits the Road. In 1979, the State of Georgia designated it the official state song.

Ray Charles, a native of Georgia, recorded a version that went to No. 1 on the Billboard magazine Hot 100.

On March 7, 1979, in a symbol of reconciliation in the aftermath of years of activism and national legislation resulting from the Civil Rights Movement, he performed the song before the Georgia General Assembly. After this performance, the Assembly adopted it as the state song on April 24.

Maurice Williams and the Zodiacs

"Stay"

"Stay" is a doo-wop song written by Maurice Williams and first recorded in 1960 by Williams with his group the Zodiacs. Commercially successful versions were later also issued by The Hollies, The Four Seasons and Jackson Browne. In 1960, the song was put on a demo by Williams and his band, the Zodiacs, but it attracted no interest until a ten-year-old heard it and impressed the band members with her positive reaction to the tune. The band's producers took it along with some other demos to New York City and played them for all the major record producers that they could access. Finally, Al Silver of Herald Records became interested, but insisted that the song be re-recorded as the demo's recording levels were too low. They also said that one line, "Let's have another smoke" would have to be removed in order for the song to be played on commercial radio

Elvis Presley

"Are You Lonesome Tonight"

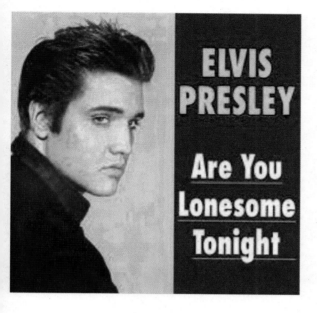

"Are You Lonesome Tonight?" In April 1960, after Elvis Presley's two-year service in the United States Army, he recorded the song at the suggestion of manager Colonel Tom Parker; "Are You Lonesome Tonight?" was Parker's wife, Marie Mott's, favorite song. Its release was delayed by RCA Victor executives, who thought the song did not fit Presley's new (and publicized) style. When "Are You Lonesome Tonight?" was released in November 1960 it was an immediate success in the U.S., topping Billboard's Pop Singles chart and reaching number three on the R&B chart. A month after the song's release, it topped the UK Singles Chart. Presley's version was certified by the Recording Industry Association of America for a Gold Record Award for 1,000,000 copies sold in the United States in 1983. It was upgraded by the RIAA to a 2xPlatinum Record Award for 2,000,000 sales in 1992.

Billboard
TOP 100
Hits

WORLD EVENTS

January

9 | Aswan Dam construction begins in Egypt. The Aswan High Dam is 4,000 metres (13,000 ft) long, 980 m (3,220 ft) wide at the base, 40 m (130 ft) wide at the crest and 111 m (364 ft) tall. It contains 43,000,000 cubic metres (56,000,000 cu yd) of material. At maximum, 11,000 cubic metres per second (390,000 cu ft/s) of water can pass through the dam. There are further emergency spillways for an extra 5,000 cubic metres per second (180,000 cu ft/s), and the Toshka Canal links the reservoir to the Toshka Depression. The reservoir, named Lake Nasser, is 550 km (340 mi) long and 35 km (22 mi) at its widest, with a surface area of 5,250 square kilometres (2,030 sq mi). It holds 132 cubic kilometres (1.73×1011 cu yd) of water.

10 | British Prime Minister Harold Macmillan makes the "Wind of Change" speech for the first time, to little publicity, in Accra, Gold Coast

12 | After seven years, a state of emergency in the British East African colony of Kenya was lifted by the Governor, Sir Patrick Renison. Proclaimed in 1952 after terrorism by the black nationalist group, the Mau Mau, the emergency regulations set curfews, restricted travel, and required the licensing of printing presses.

15 | The day after Soviet leader Nikita Khrushchev asked the Supreme Soviet of the USSR to formally approve his proposal to reduce the Soviet armed forces by nearly one-third, the 1,300 members in both houses gave their unanimous assent. The reduction, from 3,623,000 men to 2,423,000 men, had been announced by Khrushchev the day before in a speech to the joint session, with a plan to shift defense expenditures to nuclear weapons and missiles. "Should any madman launch an attack on our state or on other socialist states," Khrushchev said, "we would literally be able to wipe the country or countries that attack us off the face of the Earth."

18 | Major General Jacques Massu, the commander of the French Army in Algeria, criticized his boss in an interview with Hans Ulrich Kempski of the German newspaper Süddeutsche Zeitung. President Charles De Gaulle, who came into power with the Army's support in 1958, was outraged by Massu's statement that "Perhaps the Army made a mistake."

20 | The Soviet Union successfully test-fired the first ICBM, the R-7 Semyorka, demonstrating a range of at least 7,760 miles when it reached a target area in the Pacific Ocean. The explosion on impact, at 8:05 pm Moscow time (1705 GMT, 12:05 pm EST), was observed by the crew of a Qantas aircraft

January

21 | In the third worst mine disaster in history, 437 coal miners were killed at the Coalbrook North Colliery at Coalbrook, South Africa, when a three square kilometer section collapsed, filling the mine shaft with methane.

24 | As many as 5,000 European residents of French Algeria, including members of the French home guard, sealed off parts of Algiers and then withdrew behind the barricades. In the crisis that followed, leaders of the French Army told Prime Minister Michel Debre that they would disregard orders to attack the insurgents. When the local police clashed with the demonstrators, 24 people were killed and 136 injured.

27 | A river of lava from the Kilauea Volcano spilled over the last earthen dike that had protected the village of Kapoho, Hawai'i, and began the destruction of the town, whose 300 residents had been evacuated. By Saturday, Kapoho was gone.

31 | At Tawfiq, a skirmish between soldiers from Israel and Syria (at that time, part of the United Arab Republic with Egypt), left 12 Syrians and 7 Israelis dead. UAR President Gamal Abdel Nasser sent Egyptian troops back into the Sinai in response.

February

3 | The Senate of France voted 226–39 to allow President Charles De Gaulle to rule by decree in order to dismantle the power of French settlers in Algeria. The National Assembly had approved the measure the day before, 441–75. "We almost saw a collapse of the state last week", Prime Minister Michel Debre told the Senators, in urging passage of the measure.

4 | The Soviet Union's support of Cuba as a Communist ally was forged as Soviet Deputy Premier Anastas Mikoyan was welcomed in Havana by Fidel Castro.

7 | Laurence Slattery and Lesley Wasley, both volunteers, permitted a team of Australian doctors at the Royal Prince Alfred Hospital in Sydney to administer curare to stop their breathing, in order to demonstrate the effectiveness of various forms of artificial respiration. Among the findings were that a drowning victim's head should be placed upright, rather than to the side, to aid breathing.

8 | Queen Elizabeth II announced that her future descendants would bear her husband's name as well as her own, creating the surname Mountbatten-Windsor.

12 | Laurens Hammond, who had created the first electronic organ and a synchronous motor for the first accurate electric clock, retired from inventing.

14 | The United Kingdom signed a new treaty of protection with the Maldives, which had been a British protectorate since 1887. The Indian Ocean island group was granted independence in 1965.

17 | The United Kingdom and the United States jointly announced that a missile warning system would be constructed at the North York Moors in Yorkshire. Britain's RAF Fylingdales would join stations at Thule AFB in Greenland, and Clear AFS in Alaska as the third and final station in BMEWS, the Ballistic Missile Early Warning System.

February

21 | André Previn made the first of 51 appearances at Carnegie Hall, playing George Gershwin's Piano Concerto in F.

24 | Argentina called off its search for an "unidentified submerged object" in Golfo Nuevo. Since January 30, when sonar picked up evidence of a trapped foreign submarine, the Argentine Navy had been searching the gulf. At one point, it appeared that there were two subs below the surface, but after more than three weeks, the Buenos Aires government concluded that if there had been a foreign sub, it had escaped.

25 | After having fled to Syria, Saddam Hussein was sentenced to death in absentia by a court in Iraq, for his role in conspiring to kill Prime Minister Abdul Karim Qassim. Saddam returned to Iraq after Qassim's assassination in 1963, and did not face a death sentence again until his execution on December 30, 2006.

28 | A tip from a Soviet player helped the United States ice hockey team win the gold medal in the 1960 Winter Olympics. Exhausted from a 3–2 victory over the Soviet Union's team the day before, the Americans were losing to Czechoslovakia, 4–3, with one period left. Nikolai Sologubov suggested whiffs of bottled oxygen for quick energy, and the U.S. responded with six goals, winning 9–4.

29 | The Family Circus made its debut. Initially syndicated by the Des Moines Register and Tribune, the comic panel was created by Bil Keane, who's TV-themed Channel Chuckles was already a newspaper feature. On the first day's strip, the three children had placed a sled on top of their sleeping father, and "Billy's" line was "Guess what it's doing out."

March

3 | Pope John XXIII elevated seven bishops to the College of Cardinals of the Roman Catholic Church, bringing the number of members to a record of 85. Laurean Rugambwa of Tanganyika became the first Black cardinal, while Peter Tatsuo Doi and Rufino Santos were the first cardinals from Japan and the Philippines, respectively.

4 | At 3:10 pm, the French cargo ship La Coubre, carrying 70 tons of munitions from Belgium, exploded in Havana Harbor while it was being unloaded. A second explosion happened while aid was being rendered. Seventy-six people were killed, all but six of them bystanders, and more than 200 were injured.

6 | Four Russian soldiers, who had been adrift in the Pacific Ocean since January 17, were rescued after a 49-day search. The American aircraft carrier U.S.S. Kearsarge picked up the four men—Sgt. Viktor Zygonschi, and his men, Antony Kruckhowske, Filip Poplavski, and Feodor Ivan—who had survived seven weeks.

13 | Author Ian Fleming was a dinner guest at the home of future American President John F. Kennedy, and described to the assemblage some humorous suggestions for how James Bond would get rid of Fidel Castro, including causing Castro's beard to fall out. CIA official John Bross, another dinner guest, called agency director Allen Dulles afterward and reported Fleming's "ideas", some of which were tried later.

17 | Sculptor Jean Tinguely introduced the first piece of "auto destructive art" at New York's Museum of Modern Art. Homage to New York, composed of bicycle wheels and motors, was activated at 6:30 pm and destroyed itself within an hour.

March

19 A portion of the Great Wall of China was opened for visitors after repairs that had first been suggested in 1952 by Guo Moruo, an official in the Communist Chinese government. The section near Badaling was originally set aside for visits by foreign diplomats, and its first guest was Nepal's Foreign Minister. In 1972, television viewers in the West would see the wall at Badaling during a visit by President Nixon of the United States, and the area is now open to tourists.

21 In Buenos Aires, Ricardo Klement brought a bouquet of flowers to his wife at their home at 16 Garibaldi Street, confirming to Mossad agents that the Argentine businessman was, as they suspected, Nazi war criminal Adolf Eichmann. The Israeli intelligence service was aware that Eichmann had married on March 21, 1935, while Eichmann was unaware that he had been found after 15 years on the run. The architect of Germany's "Final Solution" genocide, Eichmann eluded capture after the end of World War II. In May, he would be abducted and brought to Israel to stand trial.

24 The Tupolev Tu-124 jet airliner, first ever to be powered by turbofans, made its first flight, at the test grounds in the Soviet Russian city of Zhukovsky. The Tu-124s were then manufactured in Kharkov, and were primarily used by Aeroflot and other Communist-bloc airlines.

25 The severed head of Oliver Cromwell, Lord Protector of the Commonwealth of England, Scotland and Ireland from 1653 to 1658, was reburied in an undisclosed location at Sidney Sussex College, Cambridge after 300 years. Cromwell's body had been unearthed after his death in 1659, with the head displayed on a spike and the rest of the corpse dumped in the sea. After being passed among several owners, the head had been kept by several generations of a family since 1815.

March

30 | A state of emergency was proclaimed in South Africa by Prime Minister Hendrik Verwoerd at 3:00 a.m., nine days after the Sharpeville Massacre, and the government began arresting dissidents. On the same day, thirty thousand black South Africans marched through Cape Town in protest of the pass laws, the massacre, and the arrest of black leaders.

31 | Several hundred political prisoners, incarcerated since the Hungarian Revolution of 1956, were released as part of the second amnesty of the Kadar regime, including playwright Gyula Háy and novelist Tibor Dery.

April

1 | R Griggs & Co. began the production of Dr. Marten's boots under license in the UK. Known as style 1460, the original product is still in production today.

7 | In an event described as "unique in world postal history", the governments of 70 nations simultaneously issued stamps to commemorate World Refugee Year.

9 | South Africa's Prime Minister Hendrik Verwoerd was shot and seriously wounded by David Pratt, a white farmer, in Johannesburg. Verwoerd survived, but would be stabbed to death in 1966.

11 | A fisherman in Masan, South Korea, discovered the mutilated body of Kim Chu Yol, a high school student who had been killed during March protests against the fraudulent presidential election. A police tear gas shell was visible in Kim's eye socket, and the outrage against the government's brutality triggered a riot. The violence in Masan was then followed by rioting in other South Korean cities.

12 | Eric Peugeot, the four-year-old grandson of French automotive tycoon Jean-Pierre Peugeot of Peugeot, was kidnapped from a playground at Saint-Cloud, near Paris. Eric was released three days later, in exchange for a ransom of $300,000.

16 | The Sino-Soviet split widened as the Chinese Communist Party journal Red Flag published the editorial Long Live Leninism, an assertion that began with the premise that the Soviet Union had, by pursuing peaceful change, deviated from Lenin's thesis that "so long as imperialism exists, war is inevitable".

April

19 More than 100,000 students in South Korea marched in Seoul in protest over election fraud committed by President Syngman Rhee in the voting of March 15, beginning the "April Revolution". Police fired into the crowds, killing 140 protesters.

21 The city of Brasilia was dedicated by President Juscelino Kubitschek, three years after he had directed construction to begin on a new capital city for Brazil. Located 600 miles inland, the city was designed by architect Oscar Niemeyer and urban planner Lucio Costa at a cost of ten billion dollars.

22 France's President Charles De Gaulle was given an enthusiastic welcome by 200,000 people upon his arrival in Washington, D.C., on the fifth day of his tour of the Western Hemisphere. President De Gaulle spoke to a joint session of Congress on April 25, urging nuclear disarmament, and was cheered by more than a million people the next day at a ticker-tape parade in New York.

29 Italy's new government led by Fernando Tambroni of the Christian Democrats, narrowly won a vote of confidence, 128–110, in the Italian Senate. Tambroni had quit on April 11, shortly after taking office.

May

3 The European Free Trade Association, founded by Britain, Sweden, Norway, Denmark, Switzerland, Austria and Portugal, came into being, five months after the Stockholm treaty signed on January 4.

6 Princess Margaret of the United Kingdom, the sister of Queen Elizabeth II, married Antony Armstrong-Jones in a royal wedding at Westminster Abbey.

7 Khrushchev surprised the world by announcing that U-2 pilot Francis Gary Powers, of Pound, Virginia, had been captured "alive and well" near Sverdlovsk, along with film taken of military bases, and Soviet currency. U.S. officials expressed "amazement" at charges that Powers had been on a spy mission.

11 The passenger liner SS France was launched at Saint-Nazaire by Madame Yvonne de Gaulle, wife of the French president.

May

15 | The Soviet Union launched Sputnik IV, a five-ton mockup of a manned spaceship, as a prelude to putting human beings into outer space. The satellite was "manned" by a heavy life-size dummy, luckily; the retrorockets fired in the wrong direction, sending the ship into a higher orbit rather than returning it to Earth. The satellite would re-enter Earth's atmosphere on September 5, 1962, with a 20-pound fragment landing at the intersection of North 8th Street and Park Street in Manitowoc, Wisconsin.

20 | In Japan, the lower house of the Diet of Japan voted at 12:17 a.m. to ratify the new security treaty with the United States, but only after police removed Socialist members who had blockaded Speaker Ichiro Kiyose in his office. Petitions against the unpopular treaty had gathered 1,900,000 names.

22 | Nearly 5,000 people were killed by a 9.5 magnitude earthquake in Chile that struck at 3:11 pm local time (1911 UTC) near Valdivia. Based on seismographic data, the tremor was measured as the largest earthquake of the 20th century, with 9.5 being almost twice as big (with almost three times as strong) as the 9.2 quake that would strike Alaska in 1964. The initial tremor killed 1,655 people, and the aftershocks killed another 4,000. Two million were left homeless, and the shock sent tsunamis that killed people as far away as Japan.

24 | Tsunamis from the Chilean earthquake, 8,000 miles away, struck the coast of Japan at Hokkaido, Sanriku and Kii, killing 119 people and washing away 2,800 homes.

25 | Four new earthquakes struck Chile, killing an additional 5,000 people.

27 | In Turkey, the army staged a coup d'état, led by General Cemal Gürsel, and arrested President Celal Bayar and Prime Minister Adnan Menderes. General Gürsel assumed both offices and replaced the legislature with 37 officers who formed the Milli Birlik Komitesi (Committee of National Unity). Menderes, Foreign Minister Fatin Rustu Zorlu and Finance Minister Hasan Polatkan were later hanged, while Bayar was released after three years imprisonment.

29 | The Monaco Grand Prix was won by Stirling Moss.

June

1 | Television was introduced to New Zealand, as broadcasts started in Auckland on AKTV, Channel 2, at 7:30 pm and continued until 10:00 pm. The first program was an episode of The Adventures of Robin Hood

2 | At a concert at the civic hall in Neston, Cheshire, John Lennon, Paul McCartney, George Harrison, Stu Sutcliffe and Tommy Moore performed for the first time under the name The Beatles.

6 | At a concert at the civic hall in Neston, Cheshire, John Lennon, Paul McCartney, George Harrison, Stu Sutcliffe and Tommy Moore performed for the first time under the name The Beatles.

10 | Earlier in the day, all 31 persons aboard Aeroflot Flight 207 were killed in the Soviet Union on an Ilyushin 14P that had departed Rostov in the Russian SFSR with four scheduled stops and a final destination of Tbilisi in the Georgian SSR. After takeoff from Sochi (in Russia) on a short flight to Kutaisi (in Georgia) and impacted at Mount Rech in the Caucasus Mountains.

June

13 | A Japanese midget submarine that had been sunk by depth charges near Pearl Harbor on December 7, 1941, was discovered after more than 18 years. The two-man I-18 was raised by the USS Current on July 6 and then returned to Japan.

18 | The Middleton Railway, at Leeds in England, became the first standard gauge line to be operated by volunteers.

21 | Armin Hary of West Germany became the first man to run 100 meters in 10.0 seconds. He was competing in an event in Zurich, Switzerland.

25 | The first talks between the government of France and the leadership of the Algerian rebel group, the FLN, took place in the Parisian suburb of Melun.

27 | Jamaican and British soldiers and policemen arrested 100 members of the First Africa Corps, a Rastafarian group, ending its influence in Jamaica.

July

3 | A bolt of lightning struck a group of religious pilgrims as they carried a statue of the Virgin Mary to the summit of Mount Bisalta, near Cuneo in Italy. Four were killed and 30 more injured.

10 | In Paris, the Soviet Union beat Yugoslavia in extra time on Viktor Ponedelnik's goal, to win the first UEFA European Football Championship, 2–1.

13 | The Pilkington Committee on Broadcasting was set up in the UK to review the state of broadcasting. After two years, the Pilkington Committee concluded that the British public did not want commercial broadcasting.

16 | The Soviet Union completed the Sino-Soviet split by notifying the government of the People's Republic of China that all 1,390 Soviet advisors and experts there would be withdrawn. Over the next month, the Soviets cancelled twelve economic and technological agreements, and 200 joint projects.

19 | Trans Australia Airlines Flight 408 was taken over by a gunman, Alex Hildebrandt of Russia, in the first airplane hijacking in Australia. The hijack was foiled when Hildebrandt was overpowered by the plane's first officer.

21 | Francis Chichester, English navigator and yachtsman, arrived in New York aboard Gypsy Moth II, forty days after sailing across the Atlantic Ocean, setting a new record.

23 | The Soviet Union launched a space capsule with two dogs, Pchelka and Mushka, in advance of manned space flight. Korabl 3 burned up upon re-entry into the atmosphere.

27 | The Republic of Ireland ended its policy of neutrality with the dispatch of soldiers of the 32nd Infantry Battalion to Africa to join United Nations peacekeeping forces during the Congo Crisis. The Defense Amendment Act 1960 had taken effect the day before after passing both houses of the Irish parliament.

August

7 | The Bluebell Railway, in Sussex, England, began regular operation as the first standard gauge steam-operated passenger preserved railway in the world.

14 | North Korea's President Kim Il-sung made his first proposal for the reunification of his nation and South Korea under a "North–South Confederation" or "Confederal Republic of Koryo". The plan, proposed again in 1971, 1980 and 1991, envisioned both nations initially keeping their political systems, with a "Supreme National Committee" to guide cultural and economic development.

16 | After 82 years as a British colony, the Mediterranean island of Cyprus was proclaimed independent by its last British Governor, Sir Hugh Foot. The new state, populated by Cypriots of Greek and Turkish descent, had Greek Cypriot Archbishop Makarios III as its President, and Turkish Cypriot Fazıl Küçük as its Vice-President. The Sovereign Base Areas of Akrotiri and Dhekelia would remain as British Overseas Territories.

18 | A French Navy bomber exploded over Morocco, killing all 27 persons on board.

24 | The "coldest temperature recorded on Earth" was measured at the −88.3 °C (−126.9 °F) at the Soviet Vostok Station. The current record low is −89.2 °C (−129 °F), recorded at the same station on July 21, 1983

25 | The 1960 Summer Olympics opened in Rome, with a record 5,348 athletes from 83 nations competing. Cross-country champion Giancarlo Peris lit the Olympic flame after Italy's President Giovanni Gronchi declared the Games of the 17th Olympiad open. Competition continued until September 11.

August

27 | In the final of the Women's 200 meter breaststroke at the Olympics, British swimmer Anita Lonsbrough broke the world record with a time of 2:49.5, a 1⁄2 second ahead of West Germany's Wiltrud Urselmann.

29 | Air France Flight 343, a Lockheed L-1049 Super Constellation airliner on a flight from Paris, crashed into the Atlantic Ocean while attempting to land during a torrential rain at Dakar in Senegal, killing all 63 persons on board.

September

4 | Before a crowd of 100,000 at the Santiago Bernabéu Stadium, Real Madrid of Spain defeated Peñarol of Uruguay, 5 to 1, to win the first Intercontinental Cup soccer football championship. The Intercontinental Cup was the product of an agreement between UEFA and CONMEBOL to create a faceoff between the winners of the European Champions' Cup and the new South American club championship, the Copa Libertadores; as with the continental championships, the intercontinental winner was being determined by the aggregate score of two matches, one in each club's home field. In the first match, played at Montevideo on July 3, Uruguayan and Spanish teams had a 0 to 0 draw.

9 | At the 1960 Summer Olympics, India's men field hockey team was defeated for the first time ever in Olympic competition, as Nasir Ahmad gave Pakistan scored a goal for a 1–0 upset. Since 1928, India had not only won 30 games in a row, it had outscored its opponents 197 goals to 8, until meeting Pakistan in the finals.

10 | ITV inaugurated regular television broadcasts of English professional soccer football matches, starting with the telecast of a Football League First Division match between Blackpool and visiting Bolton Wanderers. The Wanderers won the match, 1-0.

13 | A total eclipse of the Moon took place and was visible in much of the Pacific Ocean. Astronomer William M. Sinton used the opportunity to make infrared pyrometric scans of the temperature of the lunar surface. Sinton confirmed findings, made by Richard W. Shorthill during the eclipse of March 13 that the Tycho crater had a significantly higher temperature than the area around it.

16 | Two dogs, Pal'ma and Malek, were launched into space aboard an R-2 rocket by the USSR.

22 | Stanley William Fitzgerald, who had been placed on the FBI's Ten Most Wanted Fugitives only two days earlier, was arrested in Portland, Oregon, after a citizen recognized him from a photograph in a newspaper.

26 | Austrian Airlines Flight 901 from Vienna crashed while making its approach to Moscow, after having stopped in Warsaw. Only six of the 37 persons on board (6 passengers and 1 crew) survived.

28 | In Cuba, Fidel Castro created the "CDRs"—"Comites para la Defensa de la Revolucion" ("Committees for the Defense of the Revolution")—with volunteers reporting to the government about any counterrevolutionary behavior by their neighbors'. Officially, there were more than 100,000 CDRs and 88% of the adult Cuban population was members in 1996.

October

2	Methicillin-resistant Staphylococcus aureus, the antibiotic-resistant form of bacteria known as MRSA, was first isolated. Dr. M. Patricia Jevons, of the Staphylococcus Reference Laboratory in Colindale, London, found the resistant form in six of 5,440 strains supplied from hospitals in southeastern England. On October 2, "Patient A" had an infection following a nephrectomy, and on the same ward, "Nurse B" had an infected skin lesion. Her findings were published in the British Medical Journal as correspondence on January 14, 1961.
6	Spartacus, directed by Stanley Kubrick and starring Kirk Douglas in the title role, premiered at the DeMille Theatre in New York City before being released nationwide the next day. The film would become the highest money earner of the year.
8	The Queen Fabiola Mountains, an Antarctic mountain group 30 miles in length, were discovered, as part of the Belgian Antarctic Expedition.
12	In a famous protest, Soviet leader Nikita Khrushchev removed his right shoe during a debate at the U.N. General Assembly, and pounded it on the table during a discussion of Soviet Union policy toward Eastern Europe. Khrushchev was angered by a remark by Philippine delegate Lorenzo Sumulong.
14	The Warragamba Dam, completed after 12 years, opened by the Premier of New South Wales.
21	HMS Dreadnought, the United Kingdom's first nuclear submarine, was launched at Barrow-in-Furness. A crowd of 11,000 gathered on Trafalgar Day to watch Queen Elizabeth II christen the sub.
24	Fidel Castro's government confiscated most of the remaining valuable American-owned businesses in Cuba to retaliate for the United States' embargo on most exports to Cuba.
25	Two petroleum barges collided with a pillar of the Severn Railway Bridge in heavy fog, collapsing the bridge and killing five people.

27	The Food for Peace program was created by unanimous vote of the U.N. General Assembly, providing for nations with food surpluses to supply "the largest practicable quantities" to nations in need, "at low cost, payable in local currencies".

November

1 | Prime Minister Macmillan of the United Kingdom announced that American nuclear submarines would be based at the Holy Loch, on the Firth of Clyde at Scotland.

2 | A jury in London concluded that Penguin Books had not broken Britain's Obscene Publications Act, clearing the way for the sale, in the United Kingdom, of 200,000 paperback copies of the book Lady Chatterley's Lover.

5 | The People's Republic of China successfully built and launched its first ballistic missile, basing it upon a Soviet weapon. The R-2, known popularly as the silkworm missile, had a range of 350 miles.

11 | RMS Britannic, the last of the ocean liners of the White Star Line, sailed from Liverpool to New York City on its last voyage. Operated by Cunard Line since 1934, the Britannic was sold for scrap three weeks later.

13 | A fire at a movie theatre in the Kurdish village of Amuda, Syria, killed 152 children who had been watching an "educational film". Some sources claim that the fire had been set by Syrian security forces.

19 | The Hawker Siddeley P.1127, the first V/STOL jet aircraft (vertical short take-off and landing) capability, made its first untethered flight. Test pilot Bill Bedford lifted, hovered, and landed the jet at the Royal Aircraft Establishment ground at Thurleigh.

26 | In elections for New Zealand Parliament, the National Party, led by Keith Holyoake, gained control of Parliament, gaining 7 seats from Prime Minister Walter Nash's Labor Party, and taking a 46–34 majority. Holyoake would take office as Prime Minister on December 12, and serve until 1972.

29 | The V-1000, the Soviet Union's first anti-ballistic missile, scored its first success, intercepting and destroying an incoming R-5 Pobeda missile in a test at Sary Shagan.

30 | Gary Lineker, English footballer and sports broadcaster, in Leicester.

December

1 Sputnik 6, a 5-ton Soviet satellite, was launched into orbit with two dogs, Pchelka ("Little Bee") and Mushka ("Little Fly"), plus mice, insects and plants. The next day, the capsule was reported to have burned up on re-entry into the atmosphere at too steep an angle. According to later reports, a self-destruct system had been built to destroy the satellite if it did not re-enter at the correct time, in order to prevent it from landing outside of the Soviet Union.

3 Camelot, the most expensive theatrical production to that time, made its Broadway debut, at the Majestic Theatre, with Richard Burton as King Arthur and Julie Andrews as Lady Guinevere.

4 The Islamic Republic of Mauritania had applied to be the 100th member of the United Nations, but the request was vetoed in the Security Council by the Soviet Union, on grounds that Mongolia had been denied admission. In 1961, Sierra Leone would become the 100th member, followed by Mongolia and Mauritania.

9 The first episode of the long-running ITV drama Coronation Street aired. It was originally planned to be a 16-part drama but became such a success that it is still running five times or more per week.

14 The first "Tied Test" in the history of Test cricket took place at the end of the match in Brisbane between the West Indies and Australia. At the end of the First Innings on December 10, Australia had a 505-453 lead. In the Second Innings, however, the West Indies had outscored Australia 284 to 232. When Australia's last batter, Lindsay Kline, came up for the 7th and final ball, the score had closed to 737 to 737. Kline hit the ball bowled by Wes Hall, and Ian Meckiff dashed toward the wicket for what would have been the winning run, but Joe Solomon fielded the ball and hit the stumps for the last out. "Until today," Percy Beames wrote in Melbourne's newspaper The Age, "there had not been a tie in Test cricket."

15 In a royal wedding at the St. Michael and St. Gudula Cathedral in Brussels, King Baudouin of Belgium married Doña Fabiola de Mora y Aragon. Earlier in the day, the two had married in a private civil ceremony at the royal palace, followed by the church wedding.

21 Major Richard Baer, commandant of the Auschwitz concentration camp, was arrested after 15 years on the run. Baer had been posing as "Karl Neuman", a gardener on the estate of Otto Von Bismarck, since 1945.

25 An earthquake occurred at Cape Otway, Victoria, Australia, magnitude 5.3, waking residents on Christmas morning at 2:42 am. Earthquakes of this size are fairly common in Victoria.

27 After being forced to leave West Germany, The Beatles made a triumphant return to Liverpool, playing at the ballroom at the Litherland town hall. Author Hunter Davies, who wrote the authorized biography of the band, commented that "If it is possible to say that any date was the watershed, this was it. All their development, all their new sounds and new songs, suddenly hit Liverpool that evening. From then on, as far as a devoted fanatical following was concerned, they never looked back."

31 After 12 years, compulsory national service came to an end in the United Kingdom. After the National Service Act 1948 took effect, men aged 17 to 21 could be drafted into the armed forces for an 18-month tour, followed by four years reserved duty.

PEOPLE IN POWER

Robert Menzies
1949-1966
Australia
Prime Minister

Charles De Gaulle
1959-1969
France
Président

Juscelino Kubitschek
1956-1961
Brazil
President

John Diefenbaker
1957-1963
Canada
Prime Minister

Mao Zedong
1943-1976
China
Party Leader

Wilhelm Pieck
1949-1960
East Germany
President

Jawahar Lal Nehru
1947-1964
India
Prime Minister

Luigi Einaudi
1955-1962
Italy
President

Hiroito
1926-1989
Japan
Emperor

Adolfo López Mateos
1958-1964
Mexico
President

Nikita Khrushchev
1953-1964
Russia
Premier

Hendrik Verwoerd
1958-1966
South Africa
Prime Minister

Dwight D. Eisenhower
1953-1961
United States
President

Gaston Eyskens
1958-1961
Belgium
Prime Minister

Sir Keith Holyoake
1960-1972
New Zealand
Prime Minister

Harold Macmillan
1957-1963
United Kingdom
Prime Minister

Tage Erlander
1946-1969
Sweden
Prime Minister

Frederick IX
1947-1972
Denmark
King

Adolf Schärf
1957-1965
Austria
President

Ferenc Münnich
1958-1961
Hungary
Prime Minister

The Year You Were Born 1960
Book by Sapphire Publishing

Made in United States
Orlando, FL
15 January 2022

13505381R00053